BY THE AUTHOR

Novels
Surviving Sting
Kiss Me Softly, Amy Turtle
Do I Love You?

Poetry
The Right Suggestion
Catch a Falling Tortoise
An Artist Goes Bananas

Criticism
Fiction from the Furnace
Student Guide to Philip Roth
Laughing at the Darkness
Reading *Catch-22*
Reading Toni Morrison's *Beloved*
Storytelling

Philosophy
The Philosophy of Humour

As Editor
Loffing Matters
The Tipping Point

THE ENIGMAS OF CONFINEMENT

THE ENIGMAS OF CONFINEMENT

A History and Poetics of Flash Fiction

PAUL MCDONALD

Greenwich Exchange
London

Acknowledgements

A portion of this book was written during a funded residency at the International Writers' and Translators' House in Ventspils, Latvia. The author would like to thank the State Culture Capital Foundation of Latvia for their assistance. Thanks are also due to Jonathan Davidson of Writing West Midlands, and the University of Wolverhampton's Centre for Transnational & Transcultural Research.

Greenwich Exchange, London

First published in Great Britain in 2018
All rights reserved

Paul McDonald © 2018

Printed and bound by imprintdigital.com
Cover design by December Publications
Tel: 07951511275

Greenwich Exchange Website: www.greenex.co.uk

Cataloguing in Publication Data is available from the British Library

Cover art: Berlin Abstract
(reproduced courtesy of Pexels)

ISBN: 978-1-910996-18-8

for my mother Brenda

CONTENTS

Introduction *11*

Folk Tales: Parables and Fables *13*

Jokes *19*

The Short Story *28*

The Prose Poem *39*

Brief Non-Fiction *49*

Flashes and the Far East *57*

South American Minificción *69*

A Hybrid Genre: The Emergence of Modern Flash Fiction *81*

The Poetics of Flash Fiction *97*

How Short Can a Story Be? *111*

Conclusion *114*

Selected Bibliography

Introduction

What Do We Call It?

This is a book about flash fiction, by which I mean short stories that are shorter than the average short story. How much shorter? Short enough to make the comparative brevity of the story noteworthy. Distinctions have been made between conventional short stories and even-shorter-than short stories for many years: the term that was applied to such stories in early twentieth-century America, for instance, is Short-Shorts, and miniature short stories have picked up a variety of names over the years, including: Briefs, Expresso Stories, Flash Fiction, Postcard Fiction, Quick Fiction, Sudden Fiction, and Very Short Stories. In different cultures they have different names: in South America they are most commonly termed *minificción,* but sometimes *cuentos ultracortos, minicuentos,* or *texticulos.* In China they are variously called, among other things, Minute Stories, Pocket Size Stories, Palm Size Stories, and Smoke-Long Stories. The shortest sometimes go by the name of Drabbles (100 words long), Micro Fiction (roughly 250-300), Nano Fiction (55 words), Hint Fiction (25 words or fewer) Twitterature (140 characters), and Six Word Stories. However, the term for miniature fiction that seems to have taken hold in Western popular culture is Flash Fiction, and this is why I have chosen it for the title of this book. I use it as a synonym for all of the short short story types I discuss here.

The Scope of the Book

My interest is in the miniature short story generally, not in any one particular form or type. I aim to explore its history and poetics, considering where the foundations of flash fiction lie, and its distinctive characteristics. Given the book's relative brevity, it can only really offer an overview of the topic, of course, but it covers what I feel are the most relevant issues in a way that will appeal equally to scholars, writers, and general readers.

Firstly I will address the related forms from which flash fiction emerged, including fables, parables, jokes, short stories, and prose poems, together with types of nonfiction such as brief essays and memoir. Though I am principally interested in how flash fiction has developed in Europe and North America, I will also spend some time discussing the strong traditions of miniature stories in South America and the Far East, and the influence they have had on the complexion of flash fiction globally. I will go on to discuss the current popularity of flash fiction, and its status as what some see as a hybrid genre, incorporating pre-existing forms whilst appearing to be a new and distinctive phenomenon. The concluding sections consider the similarities and differences between flashes and conventional short stories, and conclude with a discussion of the shortest flash fiction forms.

Folk Tales: Parables and Fables

Parables and fables are narrative forms with a history that goes back as long as storytelling itself, and examples can be found in the earliest extant texts. They are often discussed in relation to the development of flash fiction, principally because brevity tends to be a feature. They both originated as instructional story forms, designed to impart wisdom or teach moral lessons.

Parables

Traditionally parables are simple tales, often constructed around characters with a moral conflict. Generally they have a clearly discernible subtext communicated via a metaphor. Parables can be found in most cultures, frequently as a feature of religious narratives – in the West perhaps the best known are the Parables of Jesus, found mostly in the Synoptic Gospels of Matthew, Mark, and Luke. The parable of the Good Samaritan in Luke 10:25-37, for instance, is about a man who is assaulted and left beaten in the road. He is ignored by two passers-by, but is helped by a third, the Good Samaritan. Jesus uses this to illustrate the moral principle of loving one's neighbour. The whole thing runs to about 300 words in English translation; it is a typical parable – a succinct tale employed to reinforce a simple aspect of the Christian message.

Parable-like tales pre-date the gospels by many centuries

however. One very early story that reads like a parable is the Sumerian 'The Three Ox Drivers from Adab'. This originally appeared in cuneiform script – the earliest form of writing – and dates back to the early Babylonian period. In the original cuneiform it is around a hundred lines long (some of the sections are indecipherable or missing), but it translates to less than 800 words in English. I include a synopsis of it here:

> 'The Three ox drivers from Adab' – 1200 BC
>
> Three ox drivers from Adab were thirsty: one owned the ox, the other owned the cow, and the other owned the wagon's load. The owner of the ox refused to get water because he feared his ox would be eaten by a lion; the owner of the cow refused because he thought his cow might wander off into the desert; the owner of the wagon refused because he feared his load would be stolen. So they all went. In their absence the ox made love to the cow who gave birth to a calf who ate the wagon's load.[1]

It is like a parable in that it is designed to be morally edifying, in this instance teaching the importance of cooperation. Instead of agreeing that one person be sent to fetch the water while the others guard the livestock and provisions, the characters quarrel and go together. In their absence a calf is born who eats their wagon's load. Though it is a simple tale with an obvious moral, it has notable rhetorical features, particularly humour. It adheres to what comedians often refer to as the rule of three, for instance, with its structure around the three quarrelsome characters: this would almost certainly have given the story a humorous feel in its original context.[2] It also creates an interesting moral dilemma that

---

[1] For a translation and discussion of this tale see Alster, Bendt 'The Three Ox-Drivers from Adab', *Journal of Cuneiform Studies* 6 (1991-93): 27-38

complicates the story a little, namely: who owns the calf? As in modern miniature narratives, the power of such tales is derived partly from their brevity: they are succinctly expressive, communicating their message in a concise and impactful way.

Fables

Fables work in a similar way, although they differ from parables in that they usually involve elements of fantasy; very often they anthropomorphise the natural world, frequently presenting animals behaving like humans. The key figure in the history of fables is the Ancient Greek storyteller Aesop (c. 620-564 BCE). No fables can be traced specifically to him, and all we have in terms of biography are references to him from sources like Plato, Aristotle and Plutarch, but his name is virtually synonymous with fables. Accounts depict him as a strikingly ugly slave who died having been sentenced to death on a bogus charge of theft. It is impossible to know how many fables he actually created, and it may well be that none originated with him at all, but over the centuries numerous fables have been attributed to Aesop. It is probably best to talk of the Aesopic fable as a category of fable, rather than attempt to link specific stories to him. In trying to define the typical Aesop fable Lee Rourke suggests that:

> There are basically only two crucial ingredients to the average Aesopic fable: a) the actual events portrayed in any fable must concern themselves with the recognisable characteristics of the

[2] See for instance the discussion in Foster, Benjamin R. 'Humor and Cuneiform Literature', JANES 60 (1974), 69-85

animals involved and b) a consistent recognisable link – a
characteristic such as fear, or hubris, for example – must act as a
conduit between their actions and the moral of the fable.[3]

So in a fable such as 'The Hare and the Tortoise', the
'recognisable characteristics' are that the former is quick and
boastful, while the latter is slow but steady. There is an obvious
connection between the tortoise's characteristics and the fable's
moral lesson: slow and steady triumphs. The simplest fables often
state the moral of the story explicitly, either at the beginning (in
the form of a promythium) or at the end (called an epimythium);
the more sophisticated fables contain the moral in the body of the
narrative itself.

Parables and fables have appeared in various contexts
throughout history, and according to some commentators their
structures and characteristics can be found in modern stories and
flashes; as Rourke suggests:

> There can be seen a direct link in the structure and form of many
> of Aesop's fables with some of the most cutting edge microfictions
> published on the internet today. The same characteristic tics are
> repeated: the need for closure, omniscient explanation, the
> fabulous and the grotesque, the same authorial command and
> most importantly the intrinsic understanding of the power of
> dissemination (Rourke, 9-10).

There is indeed a 'need for closure' in many traditional fables,
which can be seen in their directness, clarity of argument, and
sense of purpose; they tend not to be intentionally ambiguous.

---

[3] Rourke, Lee, *A Brief History of Fables: From Aesop to Flash Fiction* (London:
Hesperus Press, 2011) 23-24

Rourke's reference to 'power of dissemination' relates to the fabulists' understanding of the popular appeal of the fable, and its links to pervasive human concerns. Among others, Rourke mentions Franz Kafka, James Joyce, Robert Walser and Jorge Luis Borges as key writers associated with the form in the twentieth century, whilst he sees Tania Hershman as a modern flash fiction writer of fable-like stories. Among the Hershman stories he discusses, for instance, is 'Inchworms', cited here in full:

'Inchworms' - Tania Hershman

Another day brings inchworms in to see me, in their droves, they inch so slowly, slowly forwards. I want a word, I tell them, just one word, my pilgrim self notes down it all, a code for stitching sounds together. But the inchworms bring cracked shells, twigs and things of no damn use to me.

I think in quotes as if you listened to my thoughts. You don't, you are not there, so even if I 'dreamt about you', just like that, you would not hear me. Even if I 'loved you from afar', you would not know. Even if I walked about me, room to room and 'swore undying' to you, you would not reply. At night, the moon and stars turn up to laugh at me, skimming overhead from tree to twig, and I, 'my heart so softly breaking,' ask for help, but they just head for home, and leave me, inching slowly, slowly forwards.[4]

There is clearly an anthropomorphic facet to Hershman's inchworms in their apparent gift-bearing capacity, but for Rourke it is the mythical dimension of this piece that betrays its affinities with the fable: 'a loop to something deep-rooted, some distant desire' (Rourke, 166). However, this piece has a level of complexity

---

[4] Hershman, Tania, 'Inchworms', *Pedestal Magazine* #53 http://www.thepedestalmagazine.com/gallery.php?item=6448

and subtlety that isn't often found in fables and parables, and it is clear that the fabulist elements have been transformed into something that distinguishes the modern version. In discussing the differences between parables, fables and microfiction, for instance, Holly Howitt-Dring writes:

> Whereas fables and parables use common narrative techniques, including dialogue, and simple plot or characterisation devices to create Everyman-style situations, and, in some senses, are predictable in their form and function, this is less likely in microfiction. A microfiction might instead use strong rhythms, or even rhyme itself, and veer more towards a held-off epiphany or epiphanic event than one grounded in reality ... Myth and legend can also be embedded in microfiction, and in fact this is another similarity microfiction shares with fables, parables and anecdotes, which themselves often rely on folklore, or a retelling of an oft-told tale. But microfiction does something else with the sources. It might make them more fantastical, perhaps using magic realism, extended metaphor and/or unlikely events. It may give them an ironic edge, or the ending, viewpoint or message may be different.[5]

Modern flashes tend to reinvent the traditional characteristics of the fable, and this can be seen in Hershman's story above. Unlike in a traditional fable, there is no simple moral associated with the inchworms that visit the protagonist. Inchworms are creatures associated with metamorphosis, of course, but in this story they are not going to effect the kind of transformation the heroine desires. They bring her 'cracked shells, twigs and things of no damn

---

[5] Howitt-Dring, Holly, 'Making micro meanings: reading and writing microfiction', *Short Fiction in Theory & Practice*, Volume 1, Number 1, January 2011, pp. 47-58 (49)

use', rather than the desired 'code' that might help her stitch her life together. The lyrical nature of the prose, with its repetitions and syntactic parallelism, give the theme of thwarted desire a poetic quality, but while this augments our sense of the narrative's mythic feel, there is no simple way to deduce its meaning. Thus it is more like a modern flash as Howitt-Dring defines it: there is no obvious 'epiphany or epiphanic event', and Hershman's reference to thinking 'in quotes' suggests the kind of 'ironic edge' indicative of more contemporary writing.

Jokes

Given that jokes tend to take the form of pithy, self-contained narratives, they have some obvious affinities with flash fictions; indeed, the relationship between flashes and jokes is highlighted in the existence of those anthologies that focus exclusively on comic short shorts.[6] Jokes are associated with oral culture for the most part, of course, but there is also a long history of joking on the page which reinforces the links with flashes; it is an important facet of the flash phenomenon that is definitely worth exploring.

Jestbooks

Collections of jokes in the form of jestbooks have been around since classical antiquity: certainly there is evidence that such books existed in ancient Athens four or five centuries BC, compiled and

---

[6] See for instance, Hazuka, Tom (ed), *Flash Fiction Funny: 82 Very Short Humorous Stories* (San Francisco: Blue Light Press, 2013)

used by professional jokers called 'buffoons'. Though none survive from the earliest period, we can get a sense of what these were like thanks to the existence of one joke collection from late antiquity, the *Philogelos*. The title means laughter lover or laughter addict, and the book was made 'in early Byzantine time, probably not later than the sixth century'.[7] It contains 265 jokes on a variety of topics that largely reflect the things that we joke about today, and indeed many of the jokes have a very contemporary feel. One joke reads:

> A man comes back from abroad and approaches a stupid prophet. Asking about his family he receives the answer, 'All are healthy including your father'. 'But it's ten years now my father has been dead,' the guy objects. 'Obviously you don't know who your father is,' counters the prophet.[8]

We wonder at the reality of the prophet's status as 'stupid', of course, given that he can think on his feet so quickly; he is more like a trickster-hero than the butt of a joke, and we might even be inclined to admire his ability to live on his wits. Like all jokes it depends on incongruity: in this case between what we expect from the prophet – the revelation of his incompetence – and what is actually delivered. It is a complete story, narrating a clear sequence of events, and like most stories it presents a character with a

---

[7] Bremmer, Jan 'Jokes in Ancient Greek Culture' in Bremmer, Jan and Roodenburg, Herman (eds) *A Cultural History of Humour* (Cambridge: Polity Press, 1997) 11-29; 16-17

[8] Joke number 201, Berg, William (trans), *Philogelos: Laughter Addict* (London: Yudu Media, 2001-2008) 69. The Philogelos was written in Greek and probably compiled in the fourth or fifth century AD, attributed to two authors, Hierocles and Philagrius.

problem: in this case a man who must decide whether to believe the prophet or not.

While the origins of jestbooks lie with the *Philogelos*, probably the most influential collection is the *Facetiae* (1450), assembled in the Middle Ages by a papal secretary named Poggio Bracciolini (1380-1459). As Derek Brewer suggests, it contains 'a series of scabrous, sometimes ancient anecdotes said to have risen from the gossip during the fifteenth-century equivalent of coffee breaks among the papal secretaries of Rome.' Poggio gave these gossipy anecdotes a 'literary polish', and they were avidly read at the time, generating many imitators in the years that followed.[9] We can get a feel for their literary dimension by looking at this fairly typical example:

> LXV 'The Story of Francesco Filelfo'
>
> We were among friends, and it came up for discussion what punishment should be inflicted upon unfaithful wives.
>
> Boniface Salutati said the best punishment of all, according to him, was that with which a Bolognese friend of his had once threatened his wife.
>
> And when we asked him what this might be, he said: 'There was a man of Bologna, much esteemed by his friends. He had a wife of a generous and expansive nature, and she was even once or twice very kind to me. One night I went to his house, when I heard the two of them engaged in a terrible quarrel. The husband reproved his wife for her infidelities, while the woman answered, as women usually do on these occasions, by denying everything. The husband then began to cry out in a loud voice, 'Giovanna!

[9] Brewer, Derek, 'Prose Jest-books Mainly in the Sixteenth to Eighteenth Centuries in England' in Bremmer, Jan and Roodenburg, Herman (eds) *A Cultural History of Humour* (Cambridge: Polity Press, 1997) 90-111; 91

Giovanna! I shall not beat you. I shall not strike you, but I propose to give you so many children that the house will be filled with them. Then I will leave you alone with them, and go away.'

We all laughed at this wonderful kind of punishment by means of which the stupid fellow thought to avenge himself for his wife's infidelities.[10]

Though the impact of the humour may be diminished, this is quite a sophisticated story. It takes the form of a frame tale that creates a number of ironies, the most obvious being a husband punishing his wife by making love to her. But the focus of the irony also seems to be on the primary and secondary narrators, particularly the latter, Boniface Salutati. While he discusses fitting punishments for unfaithful wives, we can't ignore the fact that 'she was even once or twice very kind to' him also! In other words, it can be read as more than a simple joke: it is a tale about hypocrisy too. Generally speaking a joke's sole *raison d'etre* is to be funny, but this story from Poggio has a degree of subtlety and depth that could be said to distinguish it, suggesting a resemblance to modern flash fiction.

Numerous jestbooks followed, one of the most famous in England being, *A Hundred Merry Tales*, printed in 1526 by John Rastell. As P.M. Zall suggests, this had something of a didactic function: 'Many of its jests are patently intended to familiarise the 'unlearned' with such mysteries as Pater Noster, the Creed, the Ave Maria, and the Seven Deadly Sins.'[11] There is a degree of realism

---

[10] *The Facetiae of Poggio and Other Medieval Story-tellers,* translated by Edward Storer, (London: George Routledge & Sons, 1928) http://www.elfinspell.com/Poggio2.html#65

in some of these jests, however, and several go to considerable lengths to create a convincing context for the humour: often they include substantial detail, developed dialogue, and phonetically transcribed speech which sometimes gives them the feel of short stories. According to Zall, the gap between the short story and the joke is first fully bridged in Thomas Deloney's translation of Des Perrier's collection *Mirrour of Mirth* (1583). This 'represents a point where jestbook and prose fiction meet ... its concern for artistic form distinguishes it as a collection of humorous short stories' (Zall, 9). Many of the jokes in *Mirrour* are around five hundred words in length, some are even longer, and they are mostly well structured and skilfully paced narratives that show clear signs of polish and refinement. One interesting piece has the lengthy title: 'Of a Doctor of degree that was so sore hurt with an oxe that he could not tell which leg it was.' It concerns a doctor who claims to have been injured when an ox brushes against the side of his gown. A surgeon is called but when he arrives the doctor can't decide if the pain is in his right leg or his left. When the surgeon touches one of his legs he screams in agony, but when the surgeon can't find anything wrong with that leg and touches the other, the doctor screams in agony again, and again the surgeon's investigation finds no signs of injury; the story closes with the following lines:

> The Surgeon perceiving that M. Doctor had no harm, but only was afraid, for to content his mind he gave it a little ointment

[11] Zall, P.M. (ed), *Introduction to A Hundred Merry Tales and Other English Jestbooks of the Fifteenth and Sixteenth Centuries* (Nebraska: University of Nebraska Press, 1963) 8

> and bound his leg with a cloth-saying unto him that the dressing would serve at that time. 'And afterward,' said he, 'Master Doctor, when you can tell me in which leg it is, another salve shall be laid upon it.' (Zall, 368)

This pleasingly understated piece is typical of the work in *Mirrour*, presenting a fully developed scene that builds to a subtle punchline. The latter doesn't reduce the story to the merely comic as is the case with many verbal jokes; rather it creates incongruity that exposes the doctor's hypochondria in a gently satirical way, acknowledging the legitimacy of his psychological trauma even as it makes fun of it. It teases rather than mocks, deftly unpacking the theme that's stated explicitly in the joke's title. While this joke, along with all of the jokes in *Mirrour*, is comparatively lengthy, brevity still plays a part in the effect it has, particularly in the impact of the final line.

Jokes and Flash Fictions

The legacy of jests can be seen in many contemporary texts that present themselves as flash fictions. Dan Rhodes's notable collection, *Anthropology and a Hundred Other Stories* (2000), for instance, collects flashes that often have a clear joke structure:

> 'Faithful'
>
> My girlfriend died. I was heartbroken, and vowed to remain faithful to her memory. At first I had no difficulty; my distress was so great that I couldn't even contemplate kissing anyone else. But, after a while, another girl started showing an interest. I resisted her advances. 'You're very pretty,' I told her, 'but it's just too soon. I'm sorry.' She wouldn't give up. She kept gently touching me and fluttering her mascara-coated eyelashes.

> Eventually I yielded, and fell into her arms. The man asked us to
> leave. He said our rustling, slurping and giggling was upsetting
> the other mourners.[12]

This flash is heavily dependent on a final line which is akin to
the punchline in a joke, undermining expectations that have been
created in the preceding narrative. Importantly, many
commentators on the aesthetics of flash fiction warn against final
lines that feel too much like punchlines because they can make
flashes appear *too* joke-like. In his advice to flash fiction writers,
for instance, David Gaffney – himself a prominent flash humourist
– points to this as a potential flaw: 'micro-stories can lean towards
punchline-based or "pull back to reveal" endings which have a
one-note, gag-a-minute feel – the drum roll and cymbal crash.'[13]
At first sight Rhodes seems to fall into this trap with 'Faithful',
although I'd suggest that it is more complex than it initially appears.
The dark subject matter alone complicates any laughter it generates.
Presumably we laugh partly because the story's title, 'Faithful',
has been rendered ironic by the punchline, where the speaker's
so-called heartbreak is comically undermined. But this might also
make us want to question what it means to be heartbroken in the
first place. The speaker tells us explicitly that he *was* heartbroken,
so on what grounds might we justifiably question that? Must we
assume that it is impossible for him to be heartbroken just because
he was unable to stay faithful to his dead girlfriend's memory for

---

[12] Rhodes, Dan, *Anthropology and a Hundred Other Stories* (Edinburgh:
Canongate, 2000) 43-44
[13] Gaffney, David, 'Stories in Your Pocket: How to Write Flash Fiction',
Guardian, 14 May, 'G2' section, 3

as long as social etiquette demands? If so, how long must he stay celibate for his grief to be authentic? We also laugh because he acts on his passion in a context that forbids it, but how does this relate to our sense of his emotional integrity? Are we laughing at him because he is immoral, or because he is emotionally inconsistent? It might be that we laugh for both of those reasons, but what does that say about us? Is the laughter born of a sense of superiority, and if so, are we justified in feeling superior? Isn't it just as likely that the laughter is associated with the taboo nature of the protagonist's behaviour? If so then perhaps we are laughing because it corresponds to something that we repress in ourselves? This potential complexity suggests that it is more than a 'pull back to reveal' narrative, and hence closer to a flash than a joke.

Humour is central to the aesthetic of the American short fiction writer Lydia Davis, and some of her shortest works also have this ostensibly simple joke structure. Consider this piece from her collection, *Can't and Won't* (2014):

> 'Ödön von Horváth Out Walking'
>
> Ödön von Horváth was once out walking in the Bavarian Alps when he discovered, at some distance from the path, the skeleton of a man. The man had evidently been a hiker, since he was still wearing a knapsack. Von Horváth opened the knapsack, which looked almost as good as new. In it, he found a sweater and other clothing; a small bag of what had once been food; a diary; and a picture postcard of the Bavarian Alps, ready to send, that read, 'Having a lovely time.'[14]

---

[14] Davis, Lydia, 'Ödön von Horváth Out Walking', *Can't and Won't* (London: Hamish Hamilton, 2014) 143

This has a number of elements that are typical of jokes. Again it employs a punchline that creates an incongruity, in this case between the notion of a hiker having a lovely time, and the image of him as a skeleton. It has immaculate comic timing too: the account of the items in the knapsack creates a delay for the final quotation from the postcard, building tension that augments the comic force of those words. It wouldn't be as funny without the preceding specific details. However, while it has an obvious joke structure, it is difficult to see it as merely a joke. The final reveal has a comic dimension certainly, but it evokes sadness as well as humour. The phrase 'Having a lovely time' creates a touching irony that humanises the hiker as he speaks to us from beyond the grave. But also it creates something of a dilemma for the character who finds the postcard: does he have a moral obligation to post it on behalf of the deceased? Something that also complicates the story is the fact that Ödön von Horváth (1901–1938) was a real person, himself a writer of fiction who actually reported having had the experience Davis relates here. How this knowledge influences our response to the piece is debatable, but it might make us reflect on Davis's right to claim authorship. She is narrating someone else's anecdote after all, and this raises questions about the nature of origin, problematizing the notion of the author as creator. Once more these elements add layers of potential meaning to the piece and lift it way beyond the level of a simple joke.

The Short Story

The Origins of the Modern Short Story

In this section I will address the development of the short story –
in other words what we might call the conventional (in terms of
length) short story as a form of fiction distinct from the novel. As
suggested above, brief stories date back to the earliest times, and
precede the practice of writing; indeed Charles May argues that
short tales predate long ones:

> [T]he wellsprings of the form are as old as the primitive realm of
> myth. Studies suggest that brief episodic narratives, which
> constitute the basis of the short story, are primary, preceding
> later epic forms, which constitute the basis of the novel.[15]

Short narratives of various kinds predate the earliest epics, let
alone the novel, and pervade history and geography. They have
been central to literature throughout its development: *One
Thousand and One Nights* (eighth century, Persia), Boccaccio's
Decameron (fourteenth century, Italy), Chaucer's *Canterbury Tales*
(fourteenth century, England) are all essentially collections of short
stories, and the majority of those stories are based on tales that
predate them by centuries. However, some argue that the modern
short story can be traced to America. American writers like Philip
Freneau (1752-1832) and Charles Brockden Brown (1771-1810)
both produced short tales in the late 1700s/early 1800s, for instance,
but, according to Fred Lewis Pattee, neither 'influenced the

---

[15] May, Charles, *The Short Story: The Reality of Artifice* (New York: Twayne
Publishers, 1995) 1

evolution of the short story' like another American, Washington Irving (1783-1859).[16] Two of his earliest and best-known stories, 'Rip Van Winkle', and 'The Legend of Sleepy Hollow', both appear in his hugely popular *The Sketch Book of Geoffrey Crayon, Gent* (1819, 1820). The book also contains essays and vignettes, but it is the stories that made its author famous, despite the fact that they were largely reworkings of pre-existing German folk tales. It is worth noting for our purposes that later editions of this book contained some *very* short pieces, including: 'A Sunday in London', 'The Inn Kitchen', and 'L'Envoy', all of which could be considered flash-length narratives at less than 800 words: indeed, as we will see, flashes have been produced alongside short stories since the emergence of the latter as a discrete form, and many of the most important figures in the history of the short story have also produced miniature narratives that fall into the category of flash fiction, and which underpin its development as a form in its own right.

There is a European influence too of course; in fact, in his useful taxonomy of the short story, the novelist William Boyd attributes the first 'modern' short story to Walter Scott (1771-1832). His story, 'The Two Drovers', was published in 1827, and Boyd argues that this is of particular importance because of how significant a literary figure Scott was. Certainly he influenced writers across the world, including those who are themselves key to the development of the short story like Irving, and perhaps even more significantly, Nathaniel Hawthorne (1804-1864). The latter's

---

[16] Pattee, Fred Lewis, *The Development of the American Short Story: An Historical Survey* (New York: Bilo and Tannen, 1923) 1

Twice-Told Tales (1837) is often cited as the first true collection of short stories,[17] and the first to prompt a critic to distinguish between short stories and novels. This critic was Edgar Allan Poe (1809-1849), himself a pioneer of the short story form. Poe's review of Hawthorne, published in 1842 in *Graham's Magazine*, identifies some of the distinctive qualities of the short story that he feels make it superior to longer forms. According to Poe, the ideal short story requires 'from a half hour to one or two hours in its perusal' because the reader is less likely to be interrupted, enhancing the intensity and 'force' of the reading experience. Though he argues that stories shouldn't be *too* short, as 'Extreme brevity will degenerate into epigrammatism', Poe praises the 'unity of effect' achievable in art forms that can be consumed at one sitting.[18] Despite his remarks about extreme brevity, some of Poe's own tales are less than 1500 words long, the shortest, 'Shadow: A Parable' reaching just under 1000, so again it is clear how willing the earliest short fiction writers were to embrace miniature fiction.

The short story was further developed by writers like Herman Melville (1819-1891) in America who, alongside producing the colossal *Moby Dick* (1851), created some of the finest short fictions of the nineteenth century. However Melville didn't particularly admire the form, and his incentive for writing them was mostly financial. Indeed the fact that the short story flourished in America in the nineteenth century is principally because a large market for

---

[17] Boyd, William, 'A Short History of the Short Story', *Prospect Magazine*, 10 July 2006. http://www.prospectmagazine.co.uk/arts-and-books/william-boyd-short-history-of-the-short-story

[18] Quoted in Pattee, *The Development*, 135.

them developed. Whereas in England periodicals would more readily serialise novels, Americans seemed to prefer complete stories, and writers could support themselves by writing short pieces. So the short form thrived in magazines like *Harper's Magazine* (established 1850), *Putnam's Magazine* (established 1853), and *The Atlantic Monthly* (established 1857); this continued into the twentieth century with magazines like *The New Yorker* (established 1925). Writers could earn huge sums with short stories, *The Saturday Evening Post* (established 1821) reputedly paying Scott Fitzgerald $4000 for one of his stories in the 1920s – naturally, as with Melville, this often meant that short story writing was more about commerce than aesthetics. Some of the key names associated with the form in late nineteenth-century America include Ambrose Bierce (1842-circa 1914), Kate Chopin (1850-1904) and O. Henry (1862-1910), all of whom are notable for having written miniature fictions alongside standard length stories. O. Henry's 1902 story, 'Of Hearts and Hands', is a mere 871 words, for instance, Chopin's, 'The Blind Man' is 755 words, and Bierce's 'The Pavior', published in 1899, comes in at a diminutive 113 words. All of these can be considered precursors to modern flash fiction, and are occasionally cited as classic flash fictions.

An enormously important influence on the modern short story in the late nineteenth century is the Russian writer, Anton Chekhov (1860-1904). He is a giant of the genre who transformed short story aesthetics; as Boyd rightly says:

> By abandoning the manipulated beginning-middle-and-end plot, by refusing to judge his characters, by not striving for a climax or seeking neat narrative resolution, Chekhov made his stories

appear agonisingly, almost unbearably, lifelike.
– William Boyd, 'A Short History of the Short Story'

Chekhov prized subtlety above all: 'one must write about the simple things,' he said, 'how Peter Semionovitch married Marie Ivanovna. That is all.'[19] Again, in terms of length, many of Chekhov's own stories fall into the category of flash fiction, including 'Rapture' (1883) and 'A Blunder' (1886) at less than 700 words each, and 'An Inquiry' (1888) at less than 950 words. The first of these, 'Rapture' (sometimes translated as 'Bliss'), is indicative of Chekhov's ability to use the miniature narrative to good effect. It starts with an excitable and unkempt young man, Mitia, running into his parents' apartment waving a newspaper and exclaiming that he is now famous. He runs all over the family home, unable to contain himself, building his parents' anticipation to the point where his father turns pale and his mother crosses herself. When his father is finally able to read the article it transpires that it refers to his son's drunkenness: he has been seen leaving a bar in a state of such intoxication that he caused an accident which made a horse bolt. The frightened horse dragged a sledge over his son's body causing a blow to the head. Nevertheless the story closes with Mitia running out of the apartment eager to convey the wonderful news of his celebrity to his neighbours. The true circumstances of the accident undermine the appropriateness of Mitia's enthusiasm, of course, but it leaves us uncertain about the source of the young man's rapture: can it really be that he is so

---

[19] Quoted in Goyet, Florence, *The Classic Short Story, 1870-1925: Theory of a Genre* (Open Book Publishers, 2014) 14
http://www.openbookpublishers.com/product/199.

happy at achieving celebrity in this way; can his life possibly be so dull and meaningless? Or is Mitia's misplaced bliss due to the blow to his head? It is an interesting piece because the dramatic way in which Mitia tells his story to his parents can be seen as a parody of the kind of storytelling that the Chekhovian aesthetic – with its emphasis on subtlety – defined itself against.

Thanks largely to Chekhov, understatement and lack of narrative contrivance became characteristics that dominated short story aesthetics until at least the mid twentieth century. His slice-of-life fictions influenced many of the important short story writers of the twentieth century, including authors like New Zealand-born Katherine Mansfield (1888-1923), and Americans such as Ernest Hemingway (1899-1961) and Raymond Carver (1938-1988).

Modernists and Postmodernists

To a large extent the evolution of the short story parallels the aesthetic developments of the novel: where writers like Chopin and Chekhov reflected a late nineteenth-century realist aesthetic, the great innovators of modernism also practiced the short form, including Gertrude Stein, Virginia Woolf, and Franz Kafka. Again, alongside their longer works, all have produced miniature narratives that would fall into the category of flash fiction. Stories like Stein's 'A Cloth', Woolf's 'A Haunted House' (1921), and Kafka's 'Poseidon' (1920) are flash-length pieces showing many of the characteristics that defined the modernist aesthetic, such as ambiguity, fragmentation, and stream of consciousness. Kafka is perhaps the most important mainly because of his sustained interest in miniature forms and the degree of critical attention they have received. He undoubtedly gave a degree of legitimacy to shorter narratives that would inspire future writers around the world. Consider this example, quoted here in full:

'Poseidon' – Franz Kafka

Poseidon sat at his desk, going over the accounts. The administration of all the waters gave him endless work. He could have had as many assistants as he wanted, and indeed he had quite a number, but since he took his job very seriously he insisted on going through all the accounts again himself, and so his assistants were of little help to him. It cannot be said that he enjoyed the work; he carried it out simply because it was assigned to him; indeed he had frequently applied for what he called more cheerful work, but whenever various suggestions were put to him it turned out that nothing suited him so well as his present employment. Needless to say, it was very difficult to find him another job. After all, he could not possibly be put in charge of one particular ocean. Quite apart from the fact that in this case the work involved would not be less, only more petty, the great Poseidon could hold only a superior position. And when he was offered a post unrelated to the waters, the very idea made him feel sick, his divine breath came short and his brazen chest began to heave. As a matter of fact, no one took his troubles very seriously; when a mighty man complains one must pretend to yield, however hopeless the case may seem. No one ever really considered relieving Poseidon of his position; he had been destined to be God of the Seas since time immemorial, and that was how it had to remain.

What annoyed him most – and this was the chief cause of discontent with his job – was to learn of the rumours that were circulating about him; for instance, that he was constantly cruising through the waves with his trident. Instead of which here he was sitting in the depths of the world's ocean endlessly going over the accounts, an occasional journey to Jupiter being the only interruption of the monotony, a journey moreover from which he invariably returned in a furious temper. As a result he had hardly seen the oceans, save fleetingly during his hasty ascent to Olympus, and had never really sailed upon them. He used to say that he was postponing this until the end of the world, for then there might come a quiet moment when, just before the end and having gone through the last account, he could still make a quick little tour.[20]

This story is quintessentially Kafkaesque, with its emphasis on an individual crushed by the kind of labyrinthine bureaucracy that epitomised modernity for the author. Poseidon may be a god, but he is reduced to the level of a frustrated office worker, unable to enjoy life. He also exhibits that key trope of modernist literature: paranoia, seen in the reference to 'the rumours that were circulating about him.' However, as with so many Kafka heroes, there is a sense in which his problem is self-made. Poseidon is disinclined to delegate any of his work because he doesn't think anyone could do it as well as him, and he is unwilling to take a different post because they are unworthy of 'the great Poseidon'. Thus he is stymied by his own ego. It is not bureaucracy alone that is the problem, then, but the protagonist's response to it. Rather like Josef K., hero of Kafka's classic novel *The Trial*, there is a sense in which Poseidon could walk away from his problem if he genuinely wanted to. His entrapment is born partly of his own obsessions, and apparent unwillingness to step outside the nonsensical logic that governs him. As in Kafka's longer fictions, then, Poseidon's situation here implies that the world we occupy is partly a world

---

[20] In Glatzer, Nahum (ed), *The Collected Stories of Franz Kafka* (London: Penguin, 1988) 434-435

we create for ourselves. It is testament to Kafka's mastery of the miniature narrative form that he is able to convey these themes with power in such a short space.

In the 1960s when the influence of postmodernism began to supersede modernism, this was again reflected in the complexion of short fiction. Postmodernists like William H. Gass (1924-2017) and Donald Barthelme (1931-1989), for instance, both produced critically acclaimed short story collections. Again many produced flash fiction-length material, particularly Barthelme who, like Kafka, is a significant figure in the development of the form. As a postmodernist Barthelme is interested in problematizing the relationship between language and reality, and this is a feature of miniature stories like 'Terminus': here an unnamed older man is having an affair with an odd, capricious young woman. She has agreed to live with him for 'a few months', at the Hotel Terminus where she spends much of her time playing a huge accordion, trying to learn 'When Irish Eyes Are Smiling'.[21] The story stresses the older man's inability to fathom either his lover, or his position in the world. Before he fell in love with her it's said that he was protected by 'irony', which had the potential to 'keep him in his right mind', but this has been eroded by the strength of his feelings for her. When she tells him she loves him he makes the mistake of believing her, but it is very difficult to trust in anything she says. Often her language is at odds with her actions, suggesting the difficulty of having faith in language. The story is characteristically playful, shot-through with absurdist comedy that generates a sense

---

[21] Barthelme, Donald, 'Terminus' in *Forty Stories* (London: Futura, 1989) 85-88 (87)

of unreality throughout; just as we cannot take his young lover's statements seriously, so we cannot take the narrator seriously either, and this underscores the point the story makes about the impossibility of fully understanding anything through language.

In Barthelme's story the brevity of the form complements its theme, throwing important elements such as irony and uncertainty into relief. It could also be said that we are more tolerant of the extreme, absurdist humour in such a short piece: it illustrates how miniature forms can be useful for experimental writers for this reason, offering an opportunity to explore ideas and styles that might become wearing in longer narratives.

New Realists, Dirty Realists, and Minimalists

In late twentieth-century America, postmodernist short stories existed alongside work that kept its focus strongly on reality: Chekhov and the realist aesthetic never lost its appeal for writers such as Raymond Carver, Tobias Wolff (1945-), Richard Ford (1944-), and many others who were termed New Realists, Dirty Realists, and Minimalists by various critics. Their writing is sometimes seen as a reaction against postmodernism, but in truth realism never went away, and has actually dominated North American literature throughout its history. The chief figure here is probably Raymond Carver, a writer principally associated with the short story. Again there are several flash fiction-length stories in his oeuvre, and his work has been anthologised in several flash fiction collections. One of his shortest is 'Popular Mechanics' (1981) at less than 500 words. This presents a scene in which a couple are splitting up: the man is in the process of packing his suitcase, and as they argue he decides that he wants to take their baby along with him. The woman picks up the infant and carries it away but he tries to take it from her and the two begin to wrestle with the baby. The story closes with the couple seemingly on the verge of dropping the baby:

> She felt her fingers being forced open. She felt the baby going from her.
>
> No! she screamed just as her hands came loose.
>
> She would have it, this baby. She grabbed for the baby's other arm. She caught the baby around the wrist and leaned back.
>
> But he would not let go. He felt the baby slipping out of his hands and he pulled back very hard.
>
> In this manner, the issue was decided.[22]

The title of the story references a magazine for engineering devotees, *Popular Mechanics*, and this may relate to the mechanics of relationships and how this couple's problems are of a kind experienced by many. It is typical Carver territory with its focus on blue-collar conflict, and it is presented in a Carveresque way with its terse, slice-of-life focus. The narrator doesn't comment on the characters' behaviour, and we have no access to their thoughts, or any real indication of how to interpret the final line. We may be meant to assume that the baby is killed, given the reference to the 'baby slipping out of his hands'; the death of the baby would obviously present a way in which the 'issue' would be 'decided', perhaps the only way. It is a very effective use of the miniature form: it is told in real time which adds immediacy to the drama, and the confined narrative space augments our sense

---

[22] Carver, Raymond, 'Popular Mechanics', *The Collected Stories of Raymond Carver* (London: Picador, 1985) 262-3

of the characters' confinement in the moment, and the intensity of their emotions.

In terms of short story aesthetics, Barthelme and Carver were at opposite ends of the spectrum, but the fact that both utilised flash-length narrative attests to the flexibility and potential of miniature forms. As we have seen, writers have employed them since the birth of the short story genre, from Irving and Poe, through Chekhov and Kafka, to the great modern exponents of the short story like Barthelme and Carver. The willingness of the highest profile authors to make use of the form surely gave it a degree of legitimacy among the broad range of younger writers who, as will be seen, increasingly embraced it in the latter part of the twentieth century.

The Prose Poem

Origins and Definitions

The prose poem is a form that is frequently indistinguishable from flash fiction, and so it is important to say something about this. It is worth beginning with a definition, and Martin Gray's is as useful as any – for him a prose poem is a:

> short work of poetic prose, resembling a poem because of its ornate language and imagery, and because it stands on its own, and lacks narrative: like a lyric poem but not subjected to the patterning of metre.[23]

[23] Quoted in Delville, Michel, *The American Prose Poem: Poetic Form and the Boundaries of Genre* (Gainesville: University of Florida Press, 1998) 2

The problem with this definition is that many texts calling themselves prose poems, like many conventional poems, make abundant use of narrative. Also, short prose pieces that don't call themselves prose poems – like flash fictions – also stand on their own, make no use of metre, and very often employ 'ornate language and imagery'. Unsurprisingly, we run into similar problems regardless of whose definition we employ, and the difficulties of generic categorisation between prose poems, poems, and stories have been much discussed by critics.

Among the earliest exponents of the form are Aloysius Bertrand (1807-1841) and Charles Baudelaire (1821-1867), and their work often looks very much like prose fiction. Consider the opening poem from Baudelaire's classic prose poetry collection, *Paris Spleen* (1869):

> 'The Stranger'
>
> Tell me, enigmatical man, whom do you love best? Your father, your mother, your sister, or your brother?
>
> > 'I have neither father, nor mother, nor sister, nor brother.'
> > Your friends?
> > 'Now you use a word whose meaning I have never known.'
> > Your country?
> > 'I do not know in what latitude it lies.'
> > Beauty?
> > 'I could indeed love her, Goddess and Immortal.'
> > Gold?
> > 'I hate it as you hate God.'
> > Then, what do you love, extraordinary stranger?
> > 'I love the clouds ... the clouds that pass ... up there ... up there ... the wonderful clouds!'[24]

---

[24] Baudelaire, Charles, 'The Stranger', Louise Varese (trans.), *Paris Spleen* (New York: New Directions, 1970) 1

Like many of the poems in the book, this can be read as a miniature story addressing the effects of modernity on the individual. The addressee is clearly alienated and longs for something beyond the unfulfilling, profit-obsessed life of the city: his celebration of beauty, and desire for something beyond his immediate environment becomes an implicit indictment of the modern world.

Let's consider another definition. The celebrated flash fiction writer Robert Olen Butler (1945-) cites desire, time and plot, as features that distinguish flash fictions from prose poems: 'it is a short short story and not a prose poem,' he tells us, when 'it has at its centre a character who yearns'. Butler argues that fiction is different from poetry because the former 'is a temporal art form' with a plot born of a character's desire.[25] But again this definition doesn't work here: Baudelaire's prose poem has all the elements of a story as Butler defines it – it clearly depicts a sequence of events that take place in time, and it focuses on a character's desire. If plot is, as Butler suggests, 'yearning challenged and thwarted', then 'The Stranger' clearly has one: as the character's celebration of clouds suggests, he longs to be 'up there' with them. As a result, while *Paris Spleen* is considered key in the development of the prose poem, it is important in the development of flash fiction too, not least because it sets a precedent for fiction writers interested in the possibilities of the miniature story as an art form, and reveals its communicative potential.

---

[25] Olen Butler, Robert, 'A Short Story Theory', Masih, Tara L. (ed), *The Rose Metal Press Field Guide to Writing Flash Fiction* (Massachusetts: Rose Metal Press, 2009) 102-105

The Further Development of the Prose Poem

Another influential volume in the development of the prose poem is Stuart Merrill's *Pastels in Prose* (1890) which translates a number of French prose poems into English, including work by Baudelaire, Bertrand, and Stéphane Mallarmé (1842-1898). This book is important because it influenced many writers working in English, including Oscar Wilde who produced a prose poetry collection of his own titled, *Poems in Prose* (1894), which in turn went on to influence other *fin-de-siècle* writers , further raising the profile of the form and demonstrating its possibilities. In the early twentieth century the spirit of experimentation associated with Modernism attracted several writers to prose poetry, including Gertrude Stein (1874-1946) and Sherwood Anderson (1876-1941), both of whom made important contributions to its development. Another influential modernist is Franz Kafka: his shorter works are often regarded as prose poems rather than short stories,[26] which again is indicative of the definition problems associated with miniature writing forms.

As the century moved on, and particularly after WW2, the prose poem became popular in America, attracting some of the highest profile American poets such as John Ashbery (1927-2017) and Charles Simic (1938-). According to one critic, 'the two main competing camps' in late twentieth-century American prose poetry 'are represented by the so-called fabulist school' on the one hand, 'and the language-oriented New Prose Poem' on the other (Delville,

---

[26] See for instance Hayman, Ronald, *Kafka: A Biography* (New York: Oxford University Press, 1982) 66

The American Prose Poem, 248). This refers to a clash in American letters between conventional prose poets such as David Ignatow and Robert Bly, and more experimental writers like Ron Silliman and Carla Harryman. The latter are allied with the L=A=N=G=U=A=G=E school of writing and their concern with language as a construction, rather than as a representation of reality. To some extent this clash parallels the dichotomy seen above between realist and postmodernist short story writers. Likewise in England, the prose poem has been championed by both mainstream and avant-garde poets. Simon Armitage's collection *Seeing Stars* (2010), for instance, falls into the former category, and often seems to bridge the gap between prose poetry and flash fiction: Paul Batchelor calls it, 'series of vignettes that hover somewhere between poetry and prose.'[27] A less conventional contemporary prose poet meanwhile is Luke Kennard, whose hilarious, *The Solex Brothers* (2005) suggests the comic influence of postmodernist fiction writers like Donald Barthelme and Richard Brautigan (1935-1984). Here is the opening paragraph from the title poem of Kennard's book:

> I boarded the train. 'It's great, the way you use your feet to play that guitar,' I said. We were all given water, a gesture some interpreted as political and, on grounds of having no interest in politics, refused to drink. 'Fools,' muttered the politician. 'Politics is in my hair. Politics is seeping out of my pores.'[28]

---

[27] Batchelor, Paul, '*Seeing Stars* by Simon Armitage', *Guardian*, 5 June 2010. https://www.theguardian.com/books/2010/jun/05/seeing-stars-simon-armitage-review
[28] Kennard, Luke, *The Solex Brothers* (Cambridge: Salt, 2007) 1

The poem goes on to relate the speaker's encounter and subsequent relationship with the eponymous Solex Brothers who, we're told, are 'twice the size of ordinary men'. It is difficult to fathom who they are or what they represent in his world, but ultimately he agrees to murder them by poisoning their gruel. Despite the surrealism and absurdist humour, the piece exhibits all the characteristics of fiction, including a character with a conflict, which here takes the form of the speaker's dilemma about how to deal with the brothers. As with fiction writers like Barthelme, Kennard's comedy is created by incongruous juxtapositions and apparent non sequiturs, and he rarely grounds his work with realism; however, it is generally underpinned by a strong narrative impulse that suggests a kinship with narrative fiction. It seldom has the lyrical intensity one might expect from conventional poetry; rather its power comes from character, comic scenes and dialogue, and it is very often closer to fiction than poetry.

Flash Fiction or Prose Poetry

Despite its affinities with fiction, Kennard's book presents itself unequivocally as prose poetry; however some writers deliberately choose not to make distinctions between poetry and fiction. Margaret Atwood's collection, *Murder in the Dark: Short Fictions and Prose Poems* (1983), for instance, leaves it up to the reader to decide which is which, presenting material that might be read either as flash fiction, memoir, parable, prose poetry, or travel writing. Likewise Russell Edson (1935-2014) is usually classed as a prose poet, but is frequently included in anthologies of miniature fiction. When asked about the question of definition in interview he said:

> 'Sudden fiction', 'micro-fiction', etc. are dodges, and even more
> artificial sounding than the term prose poem ... Poetry and fiction
> are two sides of the same coin. But neither succeeds without being
> something of the other.[29]

Edson has been extremely influential both to people who call themselves prose poets and those who prefer the term storytellers. For instance, Lydia Davis, who after winning the International Booker Prize for *Collected Stories* (2013) is probably the highest profile flash fiction writer in the world, names Edson as a major influence. She calls herself a storyteller, and her comments on her early development as a writer are worth citing:

> I was simply reacting against Edson's designation of his pieces as
> 'poems', which I have seen on the covers of his collections (more
> often than 'prose poems' or 'fables'). I might call them 'fables',
> except that this term usually implies a moral or precept, and I
> think his pieces are wonderfully free of morals. They are stories,
> for me, because they are full of narrative. The weight of emphasis
> in them is on the narrative, I think, not on the language. When
> the emphasis shifts onto the language, then maybe they enter the
> realm of poem.[30]

Davis's suggestion that fiction and poetry exist at either end of a narrative-language spectrum is probably as useful as any place to begin for those who insist on categorising. I will illustrate it by comparing two pieces by Edson; consider this first:

---

[29] Edson, Russell, 'Interview: The Art of the Prose Poem, Russell Edson', *The Prose Poem: An International Journal*, Volume 8, 1999.
http://digitalcommons.providence.edu/cgi viewcontent.cgi?article=1596&context=prosepoem
[30] 'Interview: Lydia Davis', *Believer*, January 2008.
http://www.believermag.com/issues/200801/?read=interview_davis

'Of Memory and Distance'

It's a scientific fact that anyone entering the distance will grow smaller. Eventually becoming so small he might only be found with a telescope, or, for more intimacy, with a microscope ...

But there's a vanishing point, where anyone having penetrated the distance must disappear entirely without hope of his ever returning, leaving only a memory of his ever having been.

But then there is fiction, so that one is never really sure if it was someone who vanished into the end of seeing, or someone made of paper and ink ... [31]

It would be difficult to describe this as a story because there is no character or conflict, and no temporal or geographical context for the ideas expressed. The emphasis is on language rather than narrative: language is foregrounded, for instance, via internal assonance in the second stanza 'returning, leaving ... having been'; it is foregrounded also via the similarity of the phrasing in the second and third stanzas: 'But there's a vanishing point/But then there is fiction'; and it is foregrounded still more via the lyrical phrasing in the closing sentence, 'someone who vanished into the end of seeing'. These features make us inclined to define it as poetry. Compare that poem, however, with the following, also by Edson:

'The Dog's Tail'

An old woman was absentmindedly stirring a pot with a dog's tail.

When her husband asked her about the furry stirrer she said, It's the dog's tail, it came off in my hand.

When her husband asked her what she was stirring she said

---

she didn't know, that all her thoughts were now for the dog's tail.

When her husband noticed that the dog was in the pot she said, Oh, is that where he is? I wondered where he got without his tail.

Her husband said, I'll bet he likes that, being stirred with his own tail. It's sort of like the tail wagging the dog.

The old woman said, I was just petting him, and it came off in my hand. I hope God wasn't looking.

Her husband suggested that perhaps it wasn't the dog's tail that broke off, but rather the dog that broke off ... [32]

There is *some* foregrounding of language here (as in the repetition of 'tail' throughout), but the narrative impulse takes precedence. If we employ Olson's criteria for defining a story, the husband is a character who, in a manner of speaking, 'yearns' as he desires an answer to his questions; also, the dialogue exchange takes place over time. Like characters in a conventional story, both have problems: the wife's absent-minded stirring and forgetfulness has a sinister dimension, and the husband's notion that the dog might enjoy being stirred by his own tail, together with his joke at the end, give this piece the unsettling feel of a dark fairy tale.

Both of the Edson pieces above were published in *The Double Room: A Journal of Flash Fiction and Prose Poetry*, but they clearly occupy opposite ends of the spectrum identified by Davis, with 'Of Memory and Distance' having more in common with poetry than prose, and vice versa for 'The Dog's Tail'. I would be inclined to call the former prose poetry and the latter flash fiction.

---

[32] Edson, Russell, 'The Dog's Tail', in *The Double Room: A Journal of Flash Fiction and Prose Poetry*, #5, Winter/Spring, 2005
http://www.webdelsol.com/Double_Room/issue_five/Russell_Edson1.html

So this is one way of distinguishing prose poetry from flash fiction: when the emphasis moves from language to narrative we move closer to the realm of stories. However, just to complicate matters more, some critics have seen poetical language as a defining feature of flash fiction. Joyce Carol Oates, for instance, suggests that:

> the rhythmic form of the short-short story is often more temperamentally akin to poetry than to conventional prose which generally opens out to dramatize experience and to evoke emotion; in the smallest, tightest spaces, experience can only be suggested
>
> – quoted in Shapard and Thomas 1986, p. 247

It may be true that flash fiction writers are more conscious of the rhythms of language than authors of longer prose: the brevity of the form inevitably throws the language into relief, and writers are likely to become more aware of all aspects of diction, phrasing, and structure. There tends to be an orientation toward suggestion rather than dramatization in flashes too, where space constraints preclude dramatic development. This does not mean that flash fictions cannot be dramatic – cooking a dog whilst stirring the pot with its tail is pretty dramatic after all – but the drama tends to be implied, rather than fully unpacked on the page. These questions will be considered more fully in the discussion of the poetics of flashes later in the book.

Brief Non-Fiction

The difference between prose poetry and flash fiction is frustratingly blurred, then, and the same can be said of the distinction between flash fiction and flash non-fiction. But the latter has an important bearing on the former, and any discussion of the underpinnings of flash fiction needs to address miniature non-fiction forms such as brief-essays, sketches and memoirs, all of which have a long history.

Dinty W. Moore locates the origins of the brief essay in the writings of 'the early Greek philosophers like Heraclitus, whose aphoristic meditations on human nature and politics date back to roughly 500 BC'. This tradition continued in works like Seneca's *Moral Epistles* (60 AD), and in some of the fragments that make up Sei Shonagon's *The Pillow Book* in eleventh-century Japan (discussed in the next section of this book).[33] Later notable exponents of the brief essay include the brilliant French essayist Michel de Montaigne (1533-1592), who in turn influenced the English philosopher and writer, Francis Bacon (1561-1626), whose beautifully structured brief essays appear in *Essays and Counsels Civil and Moral* (1625). In the nineteenth century some of Charles Lamb's *Essays of Elia* (1823) could be said to fall into the category of flash non-fiction, as do some of Washington Irving's pieces in his *Sketch Book* mentioned earlier.

Particularly noteworthy from the point of view of extreme

---

[33] Moore, Dinty W., 'Of Fire and Ice: The Pleasing Sting of Flash Nonfiction', in Moore, Dinty W. (ed), *The Rose Metal Press Field Guide to Writing Flash Non-Fiction* (Brookline: Rose Metal Press, 2012) xv

brevity is the work of the art critic and anarchist Félix Fénéon (1861-1944). In 1906 he demonstrated an ability to render exquisite miniature non-fictions in a series of news clippings or 'fillers' written anonymously for the French paper *Le Matin* – eventually collected into one volume titled *Les Nouvelles en Trois Lignes*, translated as *Novels in Three Lines* (2007). He would take his stories from news wire services, word-of-mouth, or from other newspapers, condensing them into two- or three-line narratives that display a remarkable talent for miniaturisation:

> On the bowling lawn a stroke levelled M. Andre, 75,
> of Levallois. While his ball was still rolling he was no more.[34]

This is typical of Fénéon's humour and epigrammatic flair. Though it is a bare-bones account of a relatively mundane incident, it manages to convey a sense of the indignity of the human condition: our helplessness in the face of mortality and contingency.

Later in the twentieth century, flash non-fiction, both in the form of essays and memoir was continued by American practitioners like James Thurber (1894-1961), S.J. Perelman (1904-1979), and E.B. White (1899-1985), and later in the century by writers such as Bernard Cooper (1951-), Eduardo Galeano (1940-2015), and Michael Ondaatje (1943-). Particularly noteworthy is Nobel Prize-winning Egyptian writer, Naguib Mahfouz (1911-2006), who presents his 1994 autobiography, *Echoes of an Autobiography*, in the form of miniature narratives: they are not so much a description of a life as a collection of mystical aphorisms

---

[34] Fénéon, Félix, in Sante, Luc (trans), *Novels in Three Lines* (New York: New York Review Books, 2007) xxvi

and parables about its essence. Indeed, miniature narrative forms tend to lend themselves well to autobiography, as Laura Tansley has written:

> [t]he short-short and the memoir seem to accompany each other so well because the fragmented, selective short-short is reflective of the fragmented nature of identity and experience, and the selective nature of memory[35]

In the twenty-first century, flash non-fiction has emerged as a discipline in its own right, as the publication of *The Rose Metal Press Field Guide to Writing Flash Non-Fiction* will attest, with outlets such as the long-running online journal, *Brevity*. In addition to such specialist journals, many of the journals that publish flash fiction also publish essays, reviews, and interviews that adhere to similar word count constraints, providing a market for modern exponents of the form. In America, the interest in miniature non-fiction was boosted at the end of the millennium by ventures such as The National Story project created by Paul Auster on National Public Radio. In conjunction with the *Weekend All Things Considered* programme, Auster solicited stories that had only two criteria: 'The stories had to be true, and they had to be short.'[36] A selection of the thousands of stories received was published as *True Tales of American Life* by Faber and Faber in 2001. As many of the reviewers pointed out, the force of the stories is inextricably

---

[35] Tansley, Laura, 'The frame within a frame: a short-short story sequence theory in a sequence of short-shorts', *Short Fiction in Theory & Practice*, Volume 1, Number 1, January 2011, 37-45

[36] Auster, Paul, 'Introduction', *True Tales of American Life* (London: Faber and Faber, 2001) xiv

related to their brevity: few of them occupy more than two pages and some take the form of the shortest anecdotes. Consider this example:

> 'The Chicken' - Linda Elegant
>
> As I was walking down Stanton Street early one Sunday morning, I saw a chicken a few yards ahead of me. I was walking faster than the chicken, so I gradually caught up. By the time we approached Eighteenth Avenue, I was close behind. The chicken turned south on Eighteenth. At the fourth house along, it turned in at the walk, hopped up the front steps, and rapped sharply on the metal storm door with its beak. After a moment, the door opened and the chicken went in (Auster, 5).

The incongruous image of a chicken behaving like a human is delightfully humorous, and the build-up to the ending is expertly managed – the repetition of the word 'chicken', for instance, augments the comic tone, as do the phrases 'hopped up' and 'rapped sharply' to describe the chicken's behaviour. The timing is exquisite, and the miniature form perfectly complements the nature of the anecdote: the piece derives its power from its pithiness.

Flash Truth, or Flash Fiction: Does It Matter?

Personally speaking, the question of whether 'The Chicken' is true or not is of little consequence to me: the tale is well rendered and engaging, and its author clearly has a flair for storytelling. The fact that most of the pieces in Auster's collection exhibit such flair might make us speculate about how much rhetoric takes precedence over reality in these so-called true stories. As Nicholas

Lezard writes in his review of the book, 'Part of the pleasure lies in allowing suspicions to take form in the background as you read. Here, after all, are the kind of moments or epiphanies on which almost all fiction hangs.'[37] While such doubts do not detract from the stories themselves, they do remind us of the potential overlap between flash fiction and nonfiction.

Alan Ziegler writes that miniature essays can 'blend memoir, observation, and opinion, often with a strong first-person voice', and are 'often akin to prose poems and short stories in length and style'; however, the thing that unites them is the claim they make to fact, offering 'the reader an explicit promise of truth – however the author defines it' (Ziegler, *Short*, xxix). The trouble with the 'truth', of course, is that it is never wholly commensurate with, or communicable via, narrative. Arguably this is particularly the case with brief narratives where authors are forced to omit much more than in longer pieces. As soon as authors begin to select which details to include in a narrative then they are, in a sense, making a fiction. Likewise, when 'observation' is blended with 'opinion' then it quickly becomes apparent that one person's opinion can be another person's fiction.

A number of avant-garde and postmodernist story writers have sought to expose the overlap between essay, autobiography, and fiction in order to highlight the inevitable interrelationships between them – see for instance Jorge Luis Borges's story, 'Borges and I', discussed later in the book. Another example is Paul

---

[37] Lezard, Nicholas, 'Would You Believe It?' *Guardian*, Saturday 12 October 2002.
https://www.theguardian.com/books/2002/oct/12/society.paulauster.

Theroux's flash fiction, 'Acknowledgements', which uses the familiar format employed by authors for offering thanks. Theroux presents his story as a list of acknowledgements, and tells us that he was inspired to write it because, in his experience, some acknowledgements prove to 'be immensely more interesting and revealing than the books themselves – nearly often they have a plot, and a little drama.'[38] Even writing acknowledgements involves shaping and manipulation: they inevitably lose their innocence in the process, and the relationship with reality becomes a little more tenuous.

Thomas Bernhard

Other writers have complicated the relationship between fiction and non-fiction in more subtle ways. The Austrian novelist and playwright Thomas Bernhard (1931-1989), for instance, blends reportage, anecdote and fiction in the stories that make up his curious collection, *The Voice Imitator* (1978, translation, 1997). Early in his life Bernhard worked as a journalist writing concise synopses of court cases and developing a talent for condensing stories that he uses to full effect here. Bernhard took much of his material for *The Voice Imitator* from newspapers, and appears to offer factual transcriptions; other stories have their origins in rumour and conversation, but even if they aren't real, they are presented as if they are. Here is one example:

---

[38] 'Afternotes', in Shapard, Robert and Thomas, James (eds), *Sudden Fiction International*, (New York: W.W. Norton & Company, 1989) 333

'True Love'

An Italian who owns a villa in Riva on Lake Garda and can live very comfortably on the interest from the estate his father left him has, according to a report in *La Stampa*, been living for the last twelve years with a mannequin. The inhabitants of Riva report that on mild evenings they have observed the Italian, who is said to have studied art history, boarding a glass-domed deluxe boat, which is moored not far from his home, with the mannequin to take a ride on the lake. Described years ago as incestuous in a reader's letter addressed to the newspaper published in Desencano, he had applied to the appropriate civil authorities for permission to marry his mannequin but was refused. The church too had denied him the right to marry his mannequin. In winter he regularly leaves Lake Garda in mid-December and goes with his beloved, whom he met in a Paris shop-window, to Sicily, where he regularly rents a room in the famous Hotel Timeo in Taormina to escape from the cold, which, all assertions to the contrary, gets unbearable on Lake Garda every year after mid-December.[39]

This man's behaviour is bizarre, but is it *so* bizarre that we would dismiss his story as a fiction? Is it any more bizarre than the true stories we see, read and hear every day? How bizarre does a story have to be before we no longer give it credence? The tale is certainly strange and funny, but what gives it power is that it reflects a recognisable feature of the human condition: a need for companionship that is so powerful that it takes precedence over reason. While it might be hard for us to imagine treating a mannequin like a human being, would it be so hard to imagine doing that with a pet? True or not, like many of the stories in the

---

[39] Bernhard, Thomas, *The Voice Imitator*, translated by Northcott, Kenneth J. (Chicago: The University of Chicago Press, 1997) 67

book it seems to tap into a fundamental reality. The reference to the man's interest in art history may also make us wonder if a love of art is any stranger than the love of this man for a mannequin. It ends with a mundane reference to the weather in Lake Garda, which in one sense returns us to normality, but also leaves us wondering what bearing the weather has on the feelings of a mannequin! It returns us, in other words, to a normality that isn't normal. The point Bernhard makes in this book is that reality often seems like fiction, precisely because it is so often absurd.

Many writers of flash fiction use reportage and anecdote as vehicles for fiction because they carry a weight of expectation about the truth status of the subject at hand. J. Robert Lennon's book of flashes, *Pieces for the Left Hand: 100 Anecdotes* (2005), for instance, has some affinities with Bernhard. In his introduction Lennon suggests that some of his anecdotes 'are true', while '[s]ome have been embellished, or fabricated entirely',[40] and the collection offers an edifying insight into reality given that we cannot determine which is which! There is a strong relationship between the anecdote and flash fiction, and many flashes take the form of anecdotes partly to exploit the assumptions we often have about their relationship with real life. Certainly many modern flash fiction writers betray the influence of Bernhard.

---

[40] Lennon, J. Robert, *Pieces for the Left Hand: 100 Anecdotes*, (London: Granta, 2005) 2

Flashes and the Far East

China

In our discussion of the forms underpinning modern flash fiction, I have so far focused principally on narratives from the West, but other cultures have strong traditions of miniature stories too. Very short stories and short prose forms have a long history in the cultures of the Far East for instance. The Chinese writer Shouhua Qi suggests that the earliest examples in China 'can be traced back as far as the creation myths of Nuwa (ca. 350 BC), Fuxi, and Pangu.' Pangu's story (AD 220-63), for instance, is a mere 350 Chinese characters.[41] Here is a synopsis:

> 'Synopsis of the Pangu myth'
>
> Pangu was born inside an egg that was surrounded by a chaotic universe. He slept in the egg for 18,000 years until he finally woke and realised he was trapped. As he forced his way out of the egg it cracked into two halves forming the Yin and Yang: the top half of the shell became the sky, the lower half the earth. He held these apart for another 18,000 years until he died, whereupon Pangu's body formed the topography of the earth, and the parasites on his corpse formed humans.

As with parables and fables, brevity is an important trait of such stories: it suits the kind of focus and straightforward drama required to appeal to the popular imagination.

The short form developed among Chinese writers like Pu

---

[41] Qi, Shouhua, 'Old Wine in New Bottles? Flash Fiction from Contemporary China', in Masih, Tara L. (ed), *The Rose Metal Press Field Guide to Writing Flash Fiction* (Massachusetts: Rose Metal Press, 2009) 15-23 (15)

Songling (1640-1715), whose *Strange Stories from a Chinese Studio* contains some 431 weird and supernatural tales, many of which translate to less than 1000 words. Qi suggests that a tradition of miniature narrative was continued by writers such as Wu Jingzi (1701-54), and Cao Xueqing (1715-63), and into the twentieth century with Guo Moruo (1892-1978) and Lu Xun (1881-1936). Here is one of the best-known examples of the latter's work from 1920:

'On Expressing an Opinion' – Lu Xun

I dreamed I was in the classroom of a primary school preparing to write an essay, and asked the teacher how to express an opinion.

'That's hard!' glancing sideways at me over his glasses, he said: 'Let me tell you a story –

'When a son is born to a family, the whole household is delighted. When he is one month old they carry him out to display him to the guests – usually expecting some compliments, of course.

'One says: 'This child will be rich.' Then he is heartily thanked.

'One says: 'This child will be an official.' Then some compliments are made him in return.

'One says: 'This child will die.' Then he is thoroughly beaten by the whole family.

'That the child will die is inevitable, while to say that he will be rich or a high official may be a lie. Yet the lie is rewarded, whereas the statement of the inevitable gains a beating. You ... '

'I don't want to tell lies, sir, neither do I want to be beaten. So what should I say!'

'In that case, say: "Aha! Just look at this child! My word ... Oh, my! Oho! Hehe! He, hehehehehe!"'[42]

---

[42] *Selected Works of Lu Hsun*, (Peking: Foreign Languages Press, 1956-60), as excerpted in Craig, Alfred, et al, *The Heritage of World Civilizations*, second edition. (New York; Macmillan, 1990), 889

http://acc6.its.brooklyn.cuny.edu/~phalsall/texts/luxun.html

The moral of this lovely story is clear: be wary of telling the truth because it is likely to land you in trouble. China's turbulent political history gives these sentiments particular power, of course, as Qi notes, 'the hearty laugh should send eerie, bone-chilling echoes across all Orwellian dystopias, Chinese and otherwise, past or present' (Qi, 17).

In the modern world flashes – or *wei xing xiao shuo* as they are known – play a significant role in Chinese literary culture, assisted by groups like the Microfiction Association of China, which was founded in 1992. Flash-length pieces are commonly used in daily newspapers and magazines in modern China, and young people in particular have been drawn to the form. There are also some journals dedicated to flashes, and several anthologies have appeared: *Selected Miniature Story Anthology with Commentaries* edited by Bo Fang-ming, for instance, was published in Shanghai, together with its sequel in 1987.[43] Increasingly Chinese flashes are becoming accessible to readers in the West via translation, and enthusiasts like Shouhua Qi have been instrumental in helping to disseminate them beyond its borders, particularly with the collection he edited in 2008, *The Pearl Jacket and Other Stories*. This book – which includes a version of Lu Xun's story above – demonstrates the diversity of modern Chinese flashes: conventional folk tales sit alongside avant-garde and postmodern texts, grouped according to the kind of themes that inform flashes worldwide: relationships, family, portraits, society, truth and art, existential

---

[43] See Ding Zuxin's comments in the 'Afternotes' section of Shapard, Robert and Thomas, James (eds), *Sudden Fiction International*, (New York: W.W. Norton & Company, 1989) 300

moments, and the strange and extraordinary. While the themes are diverse, however, as with the Xun piece above, political polemic lies beneath the surface of so many of these tales that it might be considered a typical trait.[44]

Japanase *zuihitsu*

Short forms are perhaps even more significant in the history of Japanese literature. Possibly the earliest notable form is *zuihitsu*, a short non-fiction method that is said to have its origins with Sei Shonagon (c. 966-1017/1025) and her collection, *The Pillow Book*, mentioned above. *The Pillow Book* is an assemblage of writing that documents Sei Shonagon's experiences in service at the court of Empress Teishi (977-1001). It is a fragmentary group of anecdotes, lists, gossip, verse, and remarks that are discrete in themselves, but connected by their shared context. The term *zuihitsu* roughly translates as 'follow the brush', which suggests the degree of spontaneity and fluidity associated with the form.[45] Here is one of Sei Shonagon's musings from *The Pillow Book*:

> 'Snow'
>
> It is delightful when there has been a thin fall of snow; or again when it has piled up very high and in the evening we sit round a brazier at the edge of the veranda with a few congenial friends, chatting till darkness falls. There is no need for the lamp, since

---

[44] See Qi, Shouhua (ed and trans), *The Pearl Jacket and Other Stories: Flash Fiction from Contemporary China* (Berkeley: Stone Bridge Press, 2008) 11
[45] See Chance, Linda H., *Formless in Form: Kenko, Tsurezuregusa, and the Rhetoric of Japanese Fragmentary Prose* (Stanford: Stanford UP, 1997) 46.

> the snow itself reflects a clear light. Raking the ashes in the brazier
> with a pair of fire-tongs, we discuss all sorts of moving and
> amusing things.[46]

This is typical of those sections that present the author's brief reflections on the nature of her experiences, conveyed with characteristically well-chosen details and lyricism. Such pieces are self-contained, but in juxtaposition with other fragments *zuihitsu* accumulate to create a powerful impression of the author and her world. Donald Keene writing about *zuihitsu* says, 'after reading a series of seemingly unrelated anecdotes or impressions, we may nevertheless feel a great sense of intimacy with the writer, much as if we had read his diary or perhaps an "I novel" in which he laid bare the joys and sorrows of his life.'[47] This is certainly the case with *The Pillow Book* where the writer's sensitivity and eye for significant detail create a powerful sense of place and authorial persona.

The *zuihitsu* has been part of Japanese literary history ever since *The Pillow Book*, with Yoshida Kenko (1284-1350), and later Motoori Norinaga (1730-1801) among the notable authors associated with the form. And it continues to influence contemporary writers in Japan and beyond: according to Amanda Rudd, for instance, the fragmentary nature of *zuihitsu* has affinities with the postmodern sensibility identifiable in authors such as Ching-In Chen and Kimiko Hahn. For Rudd, the latter's *The*

---

[46] Morris, Ivan (trans), *The Pillowbook of Sei Shonagon* (London: Penguin Books, 1971)
http://chnm.gmu.edu/wwh/modules/lesson2/lesson2.php?s=1
[47] Keene, Donald, *Seeds in the Heart: Japanese Literature from Earliest Times to the Late Sixteenth Century* (New York: Columbia UP, 1999) 9

Narrow Road to the Interior (2006), 'like *The Pillow Book*, is a jumble of various pieces: long and short poems containing fragments, snippets from real or imagined conversations and emails, lists, and even course syllabi and tests.'[48] The disjointed, discontinuous nature of the text mirrors the fragmentation of identity associated with postmodernity.

Haibun

While most people in the West will be acquainted with minimalist poetic forms like haiku, perhaps less are familiar with *haibun*, a form characterised by short pieces of narrative prose concluding with a haiku. Most are between one hundred to three hundred words, and include the haiku at the end, with the connections between the prose and haiku sections left unexplained. According to William J. Higginson the key characteristics of the *haibun* include brevity, abbreviated syntax, humour, detachment, and an imagistic quality that normally eschews 'abstractions or generalisations'.[49] One of the first exponents was Japanese poet Matsuo Basho (1644-1694), and perhaps the most famous of these are contained in his travel journal, *Narrow Road of the Interior* (1694), which you will note inspired the title of Kimiko Hahn's book mentioned above. Here is a good example:

---

[48] Rudd, Amanda, 'Following Where the Brush Leads: The Potential of the Zuihitsu in American Postmodernist Literature', *Plaza: Dialogues in Language and Literature*, 1, 1, 42-49, May 2011.
Available at: https://journals.tdl.org/plaza/index.php/plaza/article/view/2094, 43
[49] Higginson, William J. with Harter, Penny, *The Haiku Handbook* (Tokyo: Kodansha, 1985) 211

The sun and the moon are eternal voyagers; the years that come and go are travellers too. For those whose lives float away on boats, for those who greet old age with hands clasping the lead ropes of horses, travel is life, travel is home. And many are the men of old who have perished as they journeyed.

I myself fell prey to wanderlust some years ago, desiring nothing better than to be a vagrant cloud scudding before the wind. Only last autumn, after having drifted along the seashore for a time, had I swept away the old cobwebs from my dilapidated riverside hermitage. But the year ended before I knew it, and I found myself looking at hazy spring skies and thinking of crossing Shirakawa Barrier. Bewitched by the god of restlessness, I lost my peace of mind; summoned by the spirits of the road, I felt unable to settle down to anything. By the time I had mended my torn trousers, put a new cord on my hat, and cauterized my legs with moxa, I was thinking only of the moon at Matsushima. I turned over my dwelling to others, moved to a house belonging to Sanpu, and affixed the initial page of a linked-verse sequence to one of the pillars at my cottage.

> Even my grass-thatched hut
> will have new occupants now:
> a display of dolls.[50]

This *haibun* offers an account of the speaker's desire to roam, and his taking leave; it closes with a haiku in which he reminds himself, and us, that life invariably continues in his absence. There is a concern for the poignancy of the ephemeral in this piece that is characteristic of Basho, and it demonstrates his genius for moving swiftly to the core of his subject. The humour is also clear, as we see when Basho is replaced at the end of his residence by 'a display

---

[50] 'Narrow Road of the Interior' in *Classical Japanese Prose: An Anthology*, McCullough, Helen Craig (ed and trans), (Stanford: Stanford University Press, 1990) 522

of dolls'. This concise form has influenced numerous writers in the West, including Buddhist-inspired Beat authors like Jack Kerouac (1922-1969), and there is a thriving web presence with *Contemporary Haibun Online: A Quarterly Journal of Contemporary English Language Haibun.*

Zen Koans

Minimalist forms have spiritual associations in the Far East too, particularly in their relationship with Buddhism. Zen Buddhism, for instance, makes use of short narratives called Koans which are essentially problems posed by Zen masters to help their students toward enlightenment. Like riddles without answers, they don't lend themselves to rational solutions; their use varies among schools of Zen, but often students are given a koan by the Master and sent away to ponder it. The aim is to arrive at a response that might liberate them from their attachment to the rational, because it is only by freeing themselves from reason that they may achieve enlightenment. As Stephen Heine writes,

> Whereas some koans contain a brief story or more complex narrative, in other instances they are as concise as a cryptic couple of sentences or phrases, thus demanding a reading between the lines to discern their significance.[51]

Here is a brief Koan from Shoyo Roku's *Book of Equanimity* (1224):

---

[51] Heine, S., *Zen Koans* (Honolulu: University of Hawai'i Press, 2014) 1

'Joshu's Wash Your Bowls'

A monk asked Joshu, 'I have just entered this monastery. I beg you, Master, please give me instructions.' Joshu asked, 'Have you eaten your rice gruel yet?' The monk answered, 'Yes, I have.' Joshu said, 'Then wash your bowls.' [52]

This Koan is typically gnomic. When he asks for instruction the monk is hoping for wise counsel from the master, something that will help facilitate his goal to enlightenment. Of course, what looks like a mundane answer shouldn't be seen that way at all: far from avoiding the question, the Master is addressing it. From a rational perspective this may appear to be a negation of the monk's aspirations, but paradox is central to Zen where such negation might be seen as positive: perhaps Joshu's point is that, as a Buddhist, the monk can only achieve what he aspires to achieve by not having aspirations?

Most Zen scripture – ie the texts from which koans tend to be taken – has an anecdotal feel, and the anecdote is the primary method of communication for Zen: as Conrad Hyers has suggested, such miniature narratives tend to be more important in Zen than 'heavily symbolic ritual, or creed and confession, or scriptural canon'.[53] Humour is often central to these anecdotes too, where its function is to deconstruct hierarchy, and expose the folly of 'the ego and its desires and attachments' (Hyers, 'Humour in Zen'[54]). For Hyers one of the ways in which Zen humour functions

[52] Roku, Shoyo, *Book of Equanimity* (1224): http://www.thezensite.com/ZenTeachings/KoanStudies/Shoyoroku.pdf, 13

[53] Hyers, Conrad, *The Laughing Buddha: Zen and the Comic Spirit* (Wolfeboro, N.H.: Longwood Academic Press, 1989) 142

[54] Hyers, Conrad, 'Humour in Zen: Comic Midwifery', *Philosophy East and West*, Volume 39, no. 3, July 1989, 267-277 (270)

in Zen philosophy and method is, 'as a technique for embracing opposites'; to illustrate this he relates a Zen anecdote in which a dying master offers words of wisdom to his monks. After telling them that 'Truth is like a river', the puzzled monks ask him, 'Master, what do you mean, "Truth is like a river"?' Wearily the master opened his eyes and in a weak voice whispered, 'OK, Truth is not like a river' (Hyers, 'Humour in Zen' 271). Hyers sees this as an example of a Zen 'attempt to demonstrate the equivalence of alternative philosophical positions and countering each by the other, to reduce alternative philosophical positions to an absurdity. The intent is [...] to point up the absurdity in trying to grasp after and cling to reality by means of this or that philosophical position' (271). Numerous contemporary Western miniature fictions exhibit humour that works to this end. A good example is this piece by Charles Simic, a poet whose prose poems often resemble surreal flashes:

> I was stolen by the gypsies. My parents stole me right back. Then the gypsies stole me again. This went on for some time. One minute I was in the caravan suckling the dark teat of my new mother, the next I sat at the long dining room table eating my breakfast with a silver spoon.
>
> It was the first day of spring. One of my fathers was singing in the bathtub; the other one was painting a live sparrow the colours of a tropical bird.[55]

The notion of equivalence is clearly a feature of this story where, in the final paragraph, rich and poor parents become

---

[55] Simic, Charles, *The World Doesn't End* (New York: Houghton Mifflin Harcourt, 1989) 5

indistinguishable for the child: from his perspective both the gypsies and his legitimate parents have 'stolen' him, and this points up the absurdity of thinking in terms of ownership when it comes to human beings. At the end we don't know which of his fathers is which, and nor apparently does the speaker. Like Hyer's Zen anecdote, Simic's prose poem undermines hierarchy, suggesting equivalence between what at first might appear to be obvious opposites: real parents and illegitimate parents. This point is comically underscored by the final image of one of the fathers (we assume by the structure of the piece that it is the biological father) attempting to pervert nature by turning a sparrow into a tropical bird. This illustrates how the kind of illogical-logic that defines koans lends itself to the short form, and it is a recurring feature in modern miniature narratives like Simic's.

Yasunari Kawabata

Along with Eastern literary forms, there are a number of individuals who have also had a significant influence on flash fiction globally. A towering figure in the history of flash fiction in the Far East, for instance, is the Nobel Prize-winning Japanese writer, Yasunari Kawabata (1899-1972). Kawabata is best known as a novelist, but he also wrote highly condensed short stories for the majority of his career, describing them as palm-of-the-hand stories. They are diverse in theme and style – some are realistic sketches, others surreal and ambiguous – but they reflect the emphasis on narrative economy that is a feature of his oeuvre generally. One popular piece is 'A Sunny Place' (1923), which tells the story of a young man who embarrasses himself by staring too long at a young woman at the seashore. He has been trying to break the habit of doing this, and we follow his thoughts as he attempts to account for the origins of this rude behaviour. He begins to recall his blind grandfather's custom of turning his head in the direction of the south, which was a 'sunny place' and he starts to wonder, 'if the south felt ever so slightly lighter even to a blind person'. He remembers that he would stare at his grandfather's staring, worrying about his fixation on the south, and 'wanting him to face north'. The sudden recollection that he had not developed his unsociable trait 'out of base motives' fills him with joy and a feeling of moral purity: it is suggested that this moment of self-awareness has transformed the hero emotionally, and he is now in a position to begin a relationship with the young woman he has just met.[56]

Over the course of his life Kawabata wrote about 140 such pieces, and felt them to be his finest achievement as a writer. As Marian Ury writes, Kawabata's style is '[i]nsistently Japanese', and some of his stories are compared with haiku, reflecting their untypical storytelling strategies: 'less a story in the usual sense than a node of storytelling, where sounds, textures, tastes, colours, trajectories and intimations are gathered, ready to expand over an invisible canvas.' But they also have something of a modernist feel too, with their use of discontinuous time and moments of epiphany.[57]

---

[56] Kawabata, Yasunari, 'A Sunny Place' in *Palm-of-the-Hand Stories*, Lane Dunlop and J. Martin Holman (trans) (San Francisco: North Point Press, 1988) 3-4

[57] Ury, Marian, 'A Man and the Idea of Women', *New York Times*, 21 August 1988
http://www.nytimes.com/1988/08/21/books/a-man-and-the-idea-of-a-woman.html.

Often anthologised in Western flash collections, Kawabata's '[i]nsistently Japanese' approach to miniature fiction has been very influential, particularly perhaps on those writers who favour the modernist aesthetic, and the avoidance of linear plot, sentiment, and moral certainty.

South American Minificción

There is also a fascinating and influential tradition of flash fiction in South America. Here termed *minificción*, the flashes associated with this region are often notable for their extreme brevity: according to some commentators, a story can be considered a *minificción* when it is less than twenty-five lines in length – in other words anything more than a page would be classed as a short story.[58] *Minificción* gained a significant profile throughout the second half of the twentieth century in countries like Argentina and Mexico, but its development can be traced back to writers such as the seminal Nicaraguan author Rubén Darío (1867-1916), who was a key figure of the *modernismo* movement in South America. *Modernismo* relates to a group of artists who eschewed unnecessary sentimentality in their work in favour of objectivity and emotional detachment, and Darío developed an aesthetic that often embraced concision and bald symbolism. His first book, *Azul* (1888) contains both poetry and prose pieces, and a well-known

---

[58] See Shua, Ana María, unpublished talk 'Microfiction in Latin America', delivered at the Reykjavík International Literary Festival 11/9/2015. http://bokmenntahatid.is/previous-festivals/festival-2015/recordings-2015

example of his miniature prose is 'Juan Bueno's Losses', the story
of a hapless character for whom nothing goes right. As a child
Juan Bueno is mocked by his school mates, and when eventually
he marries he is beaten by his wife. One morning St Joseph happens
upon the hero as he is being beaten: he intervenes and promises to
help Juan Bueno live a happier life. Thereafter the hero constantly
asks St Joseph for help with his seemingly endless list of problems,
until eventually St Joseph loses his temper and starts beating Juan
Bueno himself! The moral is simple enough – some people cannot
be helped, and they will try the patience of a saint.

Darío's influence can be seen in the writing of authors of the
next generation such as the Mexicans Alfonso Reyes (1889-1959)
and Julio Torri (1889-1970). In his recent thesis on *minificción*,
Colin Peters suggests that Torri might be considered the author of
'the first true *minificción*' with his story, 'Circe', a piece drawing
on the myth of Odysseus and his encounter with the Sirens. I quote
it here in full:

> 'Circe'
>
> Oh Circe, venerable goddess! I have carefully heeded your
> warnings. But I did not tie myself to the mast when we made out
> the Sirens' island because I had decided to lose myself. In the
> middle of the silent sea lay the final plain: it looked like a shock
> of violets wandering through the water.
>
> Oh Circe, noble beautiful-haired goddess! My fate is cruel.
> Since I had decided to lose myself the sirens did not sing for
> me.[59]

---

[59] First appeared in *Ensayos y poemas*, 1917. This translation was performed
by Ana María Shua, during her unpublished talk 'Microfiction in Latin
America', the Reykjavík International Literary Festival 11/9/2015.
http://bokmenntahatid.is/previous-festivals/festival-2015/recordings-2015

In Homer's original, Odysseus follows the advice of the goddess Circe in having his men bind him to the mast of his ship so that he cannot be drawn by the Siren's song: when he hears it he begs to be free, but his men bind him tighter. In Torri's version the hero appears to have wanted to have been led to his death by the Sirens, but the Sirens are aware of this and so they don't sing for him. It is an interesting departure in that it might work to augment our sense of the hero's conflict, playing off his status as an occasionally tormented and contradictory individual. According to Peters, this story exhibits characteristics common to South American *minificción*, including extreme brevity, poetic phrasing, and intertextuality. It is essentially a fictional intervention which, as Peters rightly says, 'renders knowledge of the story of Odysseus, Circe and the sirens essential for the comprehension of the piece.'[60] This tendency toward allusion anticipates much of what is to follow in miniature fictions from this part of the world, and, as will be seen, from flash fiction generally.

Other important contributors to the development of form include the Argentinians, Leopoldo Lugones (1874-1938), and Macedonio Fernández (1874-1952). Neither wrote a huge amount of *minificciónes* themselves, but the former did produce an influential collection of short pieces called *Filosofícula* (1924), which includes essays, parables and poems, and often appears to blur distinctions between these forms; the latter meanwhile was a huge influence on future avant garde South American writers and

---

[60] Peters, Colin, *Minificción: A Narratological Investigation*, Magister der Philosophie (Mag. phil.). Unpublished thesis. (Universität Wien, September 2008) 9

minificción masters such as Jorge Luis Borges (1899-1986). Like Borges, Macedonio Fernández was a playful, highly experimental writer interested in themes like the boundary between dreams and reality, the myth of origins, the impossibility of originality in art, and the fluidity of identity. Fernández did occasionally use concise forms himself to explore his philosophies of fiction; one excellent example is 'A Novel for Readers with Nerves of Steel', which opens with the line:

> A Sunday rain was falling, completely by mistake, since it was Tuesday, the dry day of the week par excellence, even so, nothing was happening: the all-out strike order of things was carried out without incident.[61]

This is characteristic of his playful style, beginning with a contradictory scene where there appears to be action, and yet nothing happens. The rain is personified, apparently falling by mistake, and the 'order of things', also personified, is out on strike! It appears to qualify its assertions as the narrative progresses, so much so that any notion of progression relates mainly to the eye's movement along the lines of text, as opposed to a passage through a conventional story. It goes on to reference a bridge which 'due to an oversight ... had been built to go from one bank to the same bank of the river', and this becomes the central image of the story. This image of a bridge that merely leads back to itself parallels Fernández's use of language in the story, and its tendency to erase its own statements.

---

[61] In Ziegler, Alan, *Short: An International Anthology of Five Centuries of Short-Short Stories, Prose Poems, Brief Essays, and Other Short Prose Forms* (New York: Persea Books, 2014) 54-55

While these writers laid the foundations for *minificción*, its true flowering comes later in the twentieth century with the emergence of writers like the Guatemalan Augusto Monterroso (1921-2003), the Mexican Juan José Arreola (1918-2001), and two Argentineans, Julio Cortázar (1914-1984) and, particularly, Jorge Luis Borges. These writers began to use the form more frequently, albeit often scattered among collections of longer pieces.

Monterroso, Arreola, and Cortázar

Apart from one novel, Augusto Monterroso limited himself almost exclusively to the short story form, and he is perhaps best known in the West as the author of one of the most widely anthologised *minificciónes*, 'The Dinosaur', which appeared in 1959:

> 'The Dinosaur' – Augusto Monterroso
>
> When he awoke, the dinosaur was still there.
>
> (In Ziegler, Alan, *Short*, 122)

If nothing else this story demonstrates how effective the briefest narratives can be, particularly when it comes to generating enigmas. Certainly Monterroso's story creates questions that cannot readily be answered, the principal one being: how are we supposed to interpret the reference to the dinosaur? If the 'he' of the story is meant to be a human being, then we might assume that the dinosaur is metaphorical: as humans and dinosaurs never coexisted that scene couldn't literally have happened. As 'he' has been sleeping, and perhaps dreaming, we might feel that the reference to 'dinosaur' relates to things that cannot be repressed: the life traumas that we strive to contain in the unconscious, but which constantly resurface to plague us. Thus 'dinosaur' may not relate to anything tangible, or external to the self, but to a thing of the mind. As far as human beings are concerned, of course, even real dinosaurs are a thing of the mind – at least no one has ever seen one, and it requires an act of imagination to make them exist. Thus the story raises all kinds of interesting questions about the meaning and status of 'the dinosaur' in the world of the story, and potentially in our own lives too.

Juan José Arreola's stories are just as cryptic as Monterroso's. He wrote across genres, but his output includes three collections of short stories, the most important and influential being *Confabulario* (1952) which was translated into English as *Confabulario and Other Inventions.* He was essentially a humourist with a strong interest in the absurd, and a willingness to satirize authority, particularly religion. He extended the short story genre by his readiness to create hybrid forms, and he is someone else intent on blurring the distinction between story, essay, fable, and mock-biography. He was by no means exclusively an author of short-shorts, but brevity was certainly key to his aesthetic as a story writer.

One of the highest profile figures in South American letters is Julio Cortázar. Again he wrote across genres and was astonishingly prolific, but his collections of short stories are particularly celebrated, and include *Bestiario* (1951), *Final del juego* (1956), and *Las armas secretas* (1959). A selection was published in English as *End of the Game and Other Stories* in 1967 (translated by Paul Blackburn). One of his most famous *minificciónes*, 'A Continuity of Parks', tells the story of a man sitting at home after a busy day reading a crime novel. Here is the opening:

> Sprawled in his favourite armchair, its back toward the door – even the possibility of an intrusion would have irritated him, had he thought of it – he let his left hand caress repeatedly the green velvet upholstery and set to reading the final chapters. He remembered effortlessly the names and his mental image of the characters; the novel spread its glamour over him almost at once.[62]

As we read on we discover that the plot of his novel involves two lovers who have planned a murder, and the perspective shifts to the world of the novel itself. We see a man and a woman in the moments before the murder, and we follow the man in his journey toward the victim. At the close of the story we realise that the victim is the man sitting alone reading the novel:

> No one in the first room, no one in the second. The door of the salon, and then, the knife in his hand, the light from the great windows, the high back of an armchair covered in green velvet, the head of the man in the chair reading a novel (139).

At less than 650 words it is a succinct tale, and its apparent simplicity conceals layers of potential meaning. It is indicative of the interest many of these writers have with the distinction between fiction and reality, with the text forcing us to think about the nature of stories, and how we use them in our lives. Clearly the protagonist here, 'Sprawled in his favourite armchair', luxuriates in his ability to escape into fiction, but by the time we get to the end we are

---

[62] Cortázar, Julio, 'A Continuity of Parks', in Thomas, James., Thomas, Denise., and Hazuka, Tom (eds), *Flash Fiction: 72 Very Short Stories* (New York: W.W. Norton & Company, 1992) 137-139 (137).

reminded that this depends on an illusion which is about to be violently shattered. The ending may be absurd in the way it violates planes of reality, but it becomes an interesting metaphor for the act of reading, inviting us to remember that the enjoyment of fiction involves suspending our sense of the division between reality and fiction: that human beings have the capacity to do that is at once wonderful, and potentially perilous ...

Jorge Luis Borges

As can be seen, then, many of these writers have a philosophical interest in storytelling, something that features much in the canon of South American *minificción*. Few have explored such issues with as much intelligence and sophistication as Jorge Luis Borges, however, and he is by far the most influential of all South American writers linked to the flash form. Borges was born in Buenos Aires in 1899 and was immersed in books from an early age: his literary influences are extremely cosmopolitan and diverse, ranging well beyond South America. His erudition is evident in his writing, where we frequently get a sense of Borges as an author in dialogue with his own reading, often to the exclusion of all that's outside it. Some of his stories read more like reflections on writing than plot-centred stories as such, and his work anticipates the experiments of postmodernism in its use of 'self-conscious metafiction, indeterminacy, and unresolved contradiction'.[63]

---

[63] Williams, Raymond I., *The Postmodern Novel in Latin America: Politics, Culture, and the Crisis of Truth* (London: MacMillan, 1997) 78

In his early years Borges wrote mainly poetry, but turned increasingly to short prose forms in his thirties and forties. It was when he lost his sight in his fifties that he began to focus more and more on flash-length forms (such as parables) because they were easier to dictate. One of his most famous is cited in full here:

'Borges and I'

The other one, the one called Borges, is the one things happen to. I walk through the streets of Buenos Aires and stop for a moment, perhaps mechanically now, to look at the arch of an entrance hall and the grillwork on the gate; I know of Borges from the mail and see his name on a list of professors or in a biographical dictionary. I like hourglasses, maps, eighteenth-century typography, the taste of coffee and the prose of Stevenson; he shares these preferences, but in a vain way that turns them into the attributes of an actor. It would be an exaggeration to say that ours is a hostile relationship; I live, let myself go on living, so that Borges may contrive his literature, and this literature justifies me. It is no effort for me to confess that he has achieved some valid pages, but those pages cannot save me, perhaps because what is good belongs to no one, not even to him, but rather to the language and to tradition. Besides, I am destined to perish, definitively, and only some instant of myself can survive in him. Little by little, I am giving over everything to him, though I am quite aware of his perverse custom of falsifying and magnifying things. Spinoza knew that all things long to persist in their being; the stone eternally wants to be a stone and the tiger a tiger. I shall remain in Borges, not in myself (if it is true that I am someone), but I recognize myself less in his books than in many others or in the laborious strumming of a guitar. Years ago I tried to free myself from him and went from the mythologies of the suburbs to the games with time and infinity, but those games belong to Borges now and I shall have to imagine other

things. Thus my life is a flight and I lose everything and everything
belongs to oblivion, or to him.

I do not know which of us has written this page.[64]

This story tells of how Borges' career and fame has created
another Borges: a doppelganger who the real person struggles to
relate to. His notoriety has transformed the things that the real
Borges genuinely enjoys such as 'hourglasses, maps, eighteenth-
century typography, the taste of coffee and the prose of Stevenson'
into something that feels inauthentic: the kind of thing that a
celebrity author might say about himself for the sake of vanity.
Thus there is a sense in which Borges' fictions have made reality
seem fictional: they have made the author appear imaginary to
himself. This notion is taken about as far as it can go in the final
line, where he claims not to know which Borges is responsible for
the text we have just read. It is typical of Borges' interest in
producing narratives which seem to address themselves – the world
beyond the text seems somehow out of reach and unknowable; all
that can be understood is the attempt to contemplate it, and the
result of that contemplation can only be uncertainty.

Modern *Minificción*

One of the reasons for the popularity of *minificción* in South
American undoubtedly has to do with the fact that high-profile
writers like Borges gave it respectability. Colin Peters suggests that
by the 1970s interest in the form was becoming increasingly

---

[64] Borges, Jorge Luis, 'Borges and I', *Labyrinths: Selected Stories and Other
Writings*, Yates, Donald A. and Irby, James E. (eds) (London: Penguin Books,
1970) 282-282

apparent, and critics began to take notice: the first to make specific mention of it was the Mexican literary critic Luis Leal in his book *Historia del cuento hispanoamericano* (1971) (Peters, 16). Since then many critics have addressed it in scholarly articles and books, and thus miniature fiction has long had the kind of presence in the academy that it is yet to achieve in the West. The Mexican magazine *El Cuento* was also instrumental in popularising the form, particularly when it established its annual *minificción* prize in 1980, limiting the length of entries to 250 words. By the 1980s, many writers had begun publishing books entirely composed of *minificción*: because of their respectability, publishers were willing to print full collections where elsewhere in the world they would likely be rejected due to limited commercial appeal.

Among the best known contemporary authors of *minificción* is Argentinean Ana María Shua, who to date has published five collections exclusively devoted to the form. Selections have been translated into many languages, and her two volumes in English are *Quick Fix: Sudden Fiction* (2008) and *Microfictions* (2009). This example is drawn from the latter:

> 'Watching TV'
>
> How strange to be like this, on the sofa, watching my own face making clumsy faces on the screen. The show's not bad but my acting leaves a lot to be desired. I don't recognize my voice; and my gestures seem false, derivative, hardly spontaneous. And the strangest thing, perhaps, is that the show is live.[65]

This is typical of Shua's quirky humour, and she clearly belongs

---

[65] Shua, Ana María, *Microfictions* (2009), translated by Steven Stewart (University of Nebraska Press, 2009) 94

to the South American *minificción* tradition: with its focus on identity, for instance, the themes in this story are similar to those explored by Borges above. The speaker of Shua's piece also seems to have a sense of herself as a fiction, and she is unable to reconcile interior and exterior versions of her own persona. Like Borges she captures the strangeness we feel on becoming suddenly aware of our being in the world, and she gives it an interesting extra dimension with the image of her reflection framed in the television. As with 'Borges and I', Shua's closing words – 'the strangest thing, perhaps, is that the show is live' – complicates the distinction between performance and reality in a way that is both comic and disconcerting.

South American *minificción* didn't develop in a vacuum of course – indeed European writers like Franz Kafka had a huge influence on Borges and others – but the South American variety does often have a distinctive feel. At the risk of generalising, the things that tend to characterise it include extreme concision, humour, metafictional self-consciousness, parody, and irony. They have a tendency to collapse time and offer complete scenes rather than slice-of-life fragments, and they seem less interested in characterisation or realism than flashes in the Anglo-American tradition. *Minificción* has had a global influence on flash fiction writers, particularly perhaps on those interested in experimentation, and postmodernists such as Barthelme.

A Hybrid Genre: The Emergence of Modern Flash Fiction

One thing that should be clear by now is that flash fiction is a hybrid genre, utilising conventions from a variety of narrative traditions and cultures. Consider Viorica Patea's comments about what she terms minifiction:

> Situated at the boundary between the literary and the non-literary, narration and essay, narration and poetry, and essay and poetry, minifictions also integrate extraliterary elements and so demand a reformulation of canonical genre boundaries and definitions. Hybrid, protean and fragmentary, minifictions introduce a new simultaneity of genres and have been read alternatively as prose poems, essays, chronicles, allegories or short stories.[66]

Not really a genre in itself, but a 'new simultaneity of genres', flash fiction has a history of being read through the lens of other genres. The implication is, perhaps, that when it's not quite a prose poem, or a joke, or a brief essay, or an anecdote, or an allegory, or a chronicle, or a fable, or a parable, or a *haibun*, or a *koan*, or a *zuihitsu*, or a short story, then there is a fair chance that it is a flash fiction!

Of course the status of a narrative is heavily dependent on the context of its consumption: it should be evident from the discussion above that the same piece of work could be read as a flash, a prose poem, a joke, a nonfiction fragment, and so on, depending on how it is presented. However, while flash-length narratives have

---

[66] Patea, Viorica, 'The Short Story: An Overview of the History and Evolution of the Genre' in (1-24) Patea, Viorica (ed), *Short Story Theories: A Twenty-First Century Perspective* (Amsterdam, New York: Rodopi, 2012) 20

been around since the beginning of storytelling, and while they often transcend strict genre definition, people have begun to identify miniature stories as a distinct form, and, as will be seen, this began in twentieth-century America.

American Short-Shorts

Having said something about the historical and geographical underpinnings of flash fiction, it is time to address its emergence as a contemporary phenomenon. In the English-speaking world, a modern awareness of short-short stories (as things distinct from the average-length short story) can be traced back to early twentieth-century America. In the early 1920s, the editor of *Cosmopolitan* magazine, Ray Long (1878-1935), read Somerset Maugham's book, *On a Chinese Screen* (1922), which collects a series of notes and anecdotes taken on a trip to China, observing that some of these anecdotes worked as short stories. Long had been looking for material that readers could enjoy in *Cosmopolitan* without the distraction of 'having to hunt for the continuation [of the story] among the advertisements', and decided to commission Maugham to write stories of a similar length, 'short enough to print on opposite pages of the magazine and leave plenty of room for illustration.'[67] Between 1923 and 1929 Maugham produced over two dozen stories for Long, later collected in *Cosmopolitans* (1938). Averaging around 2000 words each, these stories are perhaps too long to qualify as flash fiction in the modern sense, but

---

[67] See Somerset Maugham's introduction to *Cosmopolitans* (New York: Sun Dial Press, 1938) vi-vii

Cosmopolitans is one of the first single-author anthologies to take shorter-than-short as a determining factor. Maugham refers to them as 'little stories' (Maugham, v), and they include some notable pieces including 'The Ant and the Grasshopper', 'Mr Know-All', and 'The Verger', all of which became the basis for later films.

The phrase 'short-shorts' in relation to miniature stories appears to have been coined by *Collier's Weekly*, which started printing stories covering half a page of their magazine in September 1925.[68] Such stories usually fell between 1000-2000 words, and became such a popular feature that numerous other magazines did the same, creating a substantial market for brief stories. The market was boosted by the emergence of a number of competitions for short-shorts, including one created by *Science and Wonder Stories* in 1929 (between 1400 and 1500 words), and, in the 30s, *Liberty Magazine* (maximum 1200 words).[69] The agent Robert Oberfirst (1903-93) was a significant figure in the early days of the short-short: he published a number of articles on the technique of writing miniature fiction, and edited a volume of such material, *Technique SELLS the Short-Short* (Boston: Bruce Humphries, Inc, 1944), which included a selection of sample stories. He is also responsible for another early collection of short-shorts, *Short-Short Stories* (1948), which includes twenty-eight of his own stories. For the most part this work was written for the popular market, and both his own writing and his advice articles reflect the importance of

---

[68] See Nelles, William, 'Microfiction: What Makes a Very Short Story Very Short?', *Narrative*, Vol 20, No. 1, January 2012, 90
[69] Tara L. Masih's introduction to Masih, Tara L. (ed), *The Rose Metal Press Field Guide to Writing Flash Fiction* (Massachusetts: Rose Metal Press, 2009) xxv-xxvi

saleability; his work tends to adhere to the 'twist-in-the-tale' formula and little of it falls into the category of literary fiction. However, in 1952 he began an annual miniature fiction anthology, *Anthology of Best Short Short Stories,* which ran till 1960, and this series published several notable authors including Jack Kerouac and Ray Bradbury (Masih, xxx-xxxi).

Flash Fiction Takes Off

A number of anthologies of short-shorts appeared in the mid-century, including *The Best Short Short Stories from Collier's* (1948) and William Ransom Wood's *Short Short Stories* (1951), but the real explosion in such anthologies comes later in the century. In 1976, a special issue of the literary journal *TriQuarterly* was published edited by Robert Coover called *Minute Stories,* including miniature works from writers like Gordon Lish and John Updike,[70] but the 1980s was the decade when the miniature really began to take off. An anthology called *Short Short Stories* (1981) edited by Jack David and Jon Redfern, aimed at the education market in Canada, collected writers like Octavio Paz and John Updike (maximum four pages); and a year later, *Short Shorts: An Anthology of the Shortest Stories* appeared edited by Irvin and Ilana Howe. This collects distinguished writers like Chekhov, Borges, and Kafka (with a comparatively high upper limit of 2500 words). More significant than either of these, however, is *Sudden Fiction: American Short Short Stories* edited by Robert Shapard

---

[70] Coover, Robert, and Anderson, Elliott (eds), *Minute Stories* (Special issue of *TriQuarterly* 35.1 (1976): 1-112), reprinted New York: Braziller, 1976.

and James Thomas in 1986, collecting stories 'of one to five pages long.'[71] The editors had noticed an increasing number of very short stories appearing in literary magazines like *The North American Review*, something they attributed in part to 'the spirit of experiment and word play in the 1960s' (xiv), and began soliciting such stories for their collection. They had a debate about what to call the form and initially suggested 'Blasters', but they abandoned this partly because it put 'too heavy, too singular emphasis on surprise' which didn't apply to their subtler pieces. The book was a success, certainly popular enough to justify more of the same over the next decade-and-a-half, including: *New Sudden Fiction International* (1989); *New Sudden Fiction (Continued): 60 New Short-Short Stories* (1996); *New Sudden Fiction: Short-Short Stories from America and Beyond* (2007); and, with Ray Gonzales, *Sudden Fiction Latino: Short-Short Stories from the United States and Latin America* (2010). What is particularly interesting about the first book is the editors' sense that the stories constituted something different from what they were familiar with as readers. As Shapard says in a 2012 article reflecting on the phenomenon:

> Some used novelistic realism but on a completely different scale. Others edged into metafiction, like Grace Paley's funny, moving 'Mother', which begins with the narrator saying she always wanted to end a story with 'and then she died', and somehow manages to surprise us, a page later, by doing so. Others accelerated absurdly like Robert Fox's luminous story 'A Fable', about a young man on the subway who is so, so happy going to his first day of work in the city that he falls in love with a pretty young

---

[71] Shapard, Robert., Thomas, James (eds), *Sudden Fiction: American Short Stories* (Salt Lake City: Gibb Street, 1986) xiii

woman seated across from him and they are married by the
conductor before the next stop. Still others ran backward, like
Hannah Voskuil's touching 'Currents', told not in flashbacks
(which return to the present) but in short paragraphs that journey
relentlessly farther and farther into the past.[72]

We've seen that miniature forms have been around since the
dawn of storytelling, but this new material felt like a departure.
For Shapard, a weight of aesthetic history informs the modern
writers' engagement with the reduction in narrative space – ancient
forms like the fable, novelistic styles like realism, modernist
experiments with time, and postmodernist metafiction are all
brought to bear on miniature narrative, creating the impression
that these stories were nothing less than 'attempts to reinvent
fiction'. He felt that the shorter the fictions, the more they
challenged conventional 'short-story characteristics'. This
prompted James Thomas, Denise Thomas, and Tom Hazuka to
reduce the word limit still more for the book that introduced the
term flash fiction in 1992: taking inspiration from Ernest
Hemingway's classic miniature, 'A Very Short Story' (1923), *Flash
Fiction: 72 Very Short Stories* (New York: W.W. Norton &
Company) included tales with an upper limit of 750 words. In his
introduction James Thomas says that they began by thinking about
stories that 'could be read without turning a page' and decided to
call them flash fictions because 'there would be no enforced pause
in the reader's concentration, no break in the field of vision', and

---

[72] Shapard, Robert, 'The Remarkable Reinvention of Very Short Fiction',
World Literature Today, 12 September 2012.
http://www.worldliteraturetoday.org/2012/september/remarkable-
reinvention-very-short-fiction-robert-shapard

hence the stories would appear in a single flash.[73] In reducing the word length the editors were responding to the fact that in the late 80s 'very short pieces, under a thousand words, [had] been appearing with greater frequency' in magazines (14). As Shapard and Thomas suggest, this in part had something to do with the increasing number of journals willing to print such material. One very important journal, for instance, was *Sundog: The Southeast Review*, edited by Jerome Stern, who also started the influential 'World's Best Short-Short Story' competition in 1986. The competition set the limit at a much shorter 250 words, and Stern used the term 'Micro-fiction' for these pieces, and for the anthology he edited in 1996: *Micro Fiction: An Anthology of Really Short Stories* (New York: Norton, 1996). This term is still often used to describe the briefest flashes.

While most commentators on the phenomenon of flash fiction cite the internet as the key factor in its development, then, we can see that a number of the most significant early anthologies predate the internet revolution by several years. However, the internet has certainly played a crucial role in augmenting the popularity of flash fiction, as will be seen.

Flash Fiction and the New Technologies

One of the contributing factors in the growth in flash fiction production and consumption has been the rise of online publication opportunities. As the number of online literary

---

[73] Thomas, James., Thomas, Denise., Hazuka, Tom (eds), *Flash Fiction: 72 Very Short Stories* (New York: W.W. Norton & Company, 1992) 12

magazines began to increase in the early-to-mid-1990s, so the market for miniature fictions suited to screen consumption expanded. In time online magazines dedicated to flash fiction began to appear, one of most influential being *Smokelong Quarterly* (established 2003), publishing work of less than 1000 words, including some of the most celebrated authors of the form. Many others have followed, and at the time of writing numerous online magazines and blogs offer regular flash fictions for free, some even offering daily stories.[74] Even those literary magazines that don't specialise in the form include dedicated flash fictions sections. Jake Freivald, who founded *Flash Fiction Online* in 2007, succinctly sums up the appeal of flash fiction for online editors in an interview with *PC World*: 'The brief nature of flash fiction makes it "Web-ready". It's long enough to tell the story [...] but not so long that people get tired of looking at the computer screen.'[75] The form complements the medium: it is easy for editors to accommodate on websites, and it suits screen sizes, even more so as they have decreased in the form of tablets and mobile phones. Also, editors like flash fictions because they can be read quickly, which is useful because submissions to literary magazines have increased hugely in the digital age. As Tara L. Marsh has noted, the new technologies enable multiple e-submission of stories to magazines, and editors are forced to contend with enormous quantities of material: '[w]hile it's always unpopular to admit this to struggling writers,

---

[74] See for instance *Flash Fiction Magazine* which publishes daily stories between 300–1000 words: http://flashfictionmagazine.com/

[75] Quoted in Pratt, Mary K., 'How Technology Is Changing What We Read' PC World (5 May 2009).
http://www.pcworld.com/article/164355/e_books.html.

reading shorter work becomes timesaving, and soliciting shorter work becomes economical' (*Field Guide*, xxxvii). As editors' workloads increase, so flash fiction offers authors a good way of catching their attention.

Flash fiction has flourished partly because it suits both readers, editors, and writers, then, but it also suits the people who teach writing. There has been an explosion of interest in creative writing on both sides of the Atlantic in recent years, which is reflected in the profusion of writing degree courses offered at universities: MFA programmes have become more common in the States, and there has been a huge increase in creative writing degrees offered by UK universities in the last twenty years. Because flash fictions are a convenient length for classroom consumption – they are employed extensively in writing workshops, they are useful for exploring a variety of storytelling strategies, and they are excellent for encouraging narrative economy. Students can read them quickly, they can be disseminated easily – often via online teaching environments – and they are less burdensome than longer stories for tutors to feedback on. As a result the numbers of people creating flashes has increased, which in turn feeds the burgeoning online outlets.

Early Facebook Fiction

As well as providing opportunities for publication, new technologies have affected the form of miniature fiction too, particularly social media. The old character limit for Facebook status updates determines the length of Lou Beach's flashes, for instance, as evidenced by the title of his collection *420 Characters.*

In the introduction he says that the status updates provided him with a daily exercise in fiction writing. He is capable of using the character limit to excellent effect, as can be seen in this example:

> The Judge sits behind the massive bench and runs his hands over the black silk robes that denote his station, his power. He caresses the fabric until he is fully aroused, then strangles the impulse to bring himself to climax. The prisoner is brought in wearing an orange polyester jumpsuit, hands shackled. He looks up at the judge, studies his face for a moment, smirks. 'This motherfucker is guilty,' they both think.[76]

This story deftly exposes the disconcerting relationship some people have with power; for this judge it has a sexual dimension which undermines his status, and unsettles us. It implies that the only thing that separates the judge from the prisoner is that the former has managed to supress his baser impulses. Certainly the two recognise each other as kindred spirits. It is an effective piece despite its brevity: we don't really need these characters to be unpacked in any more detail, partly perhaps because the story appeals to feelings most readers will have had themselves about those who crave power and status. While it is a familiar idea, and draws on stereotype, it is lifted beyond the level of cliché by the final line, 'This motherfucker is guilty', which links the two characters and reveals the moral of their story in a pleasingly succinct way.

---

[76] Beach, Lou, *420 Characters* (2010)
http://www.420characters.net/stories.html

Twitter Flashes

Twitter has also influenced the shape of brief fictions. Some Twitter story writers use the 140 character limit as a constraint that they must adhere to exactly; others use it as an upper limit and are happy if their character count is less than 140. Twitter stories usually don't have titles, which is something that distinguishes them from other flash forms, and which, as Carla Raguseo suggests, 'emphasises their fragmentary presentation.'[77] Another distinctive feature is 'the automatic time stamp published in every tweet which gives us a sense of immediacy.' A well-known exponent of the stricter, 140-character-story tweet is the Canadian author Arjun Basu. He calls his stories Twisters, and has published thousands since he began writing them in 2009.

> He was falling in love with the sad girl. He said, I want to taste your sadness. She went away and came back with a plate of scrambled eggs.[78]

This is exactly 140 characters including the full stop, and I would claim that it is a successful story. It turns on how we interpret the final image of the scrambled eggs, of course, which suggest that the woman's sadness might have something to do with a miscarriage, perhaps, or the discovery of infertility. Undoubtedly it adds an element of darkness to the narrative which qualifies the

---

[77] Raguseo, Carla, 'Twitter Fiction: Social Networking and Microfiction in 140 Characters', *The Electronic Journal for English as a Second Language*, March 2010, Volume 13, Number 4 (unpaginated)

[78] See Arjun Basu's website: http://arjunbasu.com/archives/tag/love

man's rather pretentious entreaty to 'taste your sadness'. She responds with a metaphor that adds poignancy to her sorrow and simultaneously exposes the fatuousness of his request.

So the internet has been a crucial factor in the increasing popularity of flash fiction, both in terms of distribution and aesthetics. For the last twenty years it has simultaneously fed and fuelled a growing, global interest in miniature stories. This is reflected in the huge increase in flash fiction competitions, flash fiction societies, and even the emergence of a National Flash Fiction Day in the UK, beginning in 2012 and supported by the Arts Council of England.

Important Authors

Flash fictions are not just confined to the internet of course. Alongside the success of flash fiction anthologies, several high profile contemporary authors are associated with the form, publishing single-author collections of flashes that ensure their presence in mainstream bookshops. One of America's most respected writers, Joyce Carol Oates, for instance, has often used miniature narrative: her book *The Assignation: Stories* (1989) contains 44 stories, some of which are no more than two pages long: dealing with human vices like greed and desire in domestic life, they reflect the preoccupations of her longer fiction. The Booker Prize-winning Canadian author, Margaret Atwood's *Murder in the Dark: Short Fictions and Prose Poems* (1999), includes numerous flash-length works and, as suggested earlier, elevates the status of miniature fiction by refusing to distinguish it from poetry. The bestselling author David Eggers has also championed flash fiction and published a collection of miniatures, *Short Short Stories*, as part of the Pocket Penguin series in 2005. Pulitzer Prize-winning Robert Olen Butler has authored two collections of flash fiction, including the innovative *Severance* (2006) containing sixty-two 240-word monologues from people who have just been decapitated! In the UK popularisers of the form include writers like Dan Rhodes with his collections *Anthropology: And a Hundred Other Stories* (2000), and the sequel, *Marry Me* (2013), which are both collections of flashes themed around relationships. Another writer who has done more than most to promote flash fiction in the UK is David Gaffney, and his *Sawn-Off Tales* (2006) and *More Sawn-Off Tales* (2013) have been widely reviewed and extremely influential.

We have seen how important miniature narratives are in the cultures of the Far East and Latin America too, of course, and high-profile authors of collections from this part of the world abound: their translated work feeds into the English-speaking flash culture and has been hugely significant. Among the numerous noteworthy flash writers from elsewhere in the world are the Israeli, Etgar Keret, many of whose collections have been translated into English: *Suddenly, A Knock on the Door* (2012) is a good recent example of his beautifully executed, Kafkaesque stories (see the example in the final section of this book). The Syrian writer Zakaria Tamer is a prominent author of flashes too: *Tigers on the Tenth Day* (1978), translated into English in 1985, for instance, contains thirty-four flashes informed by the author's characteristic fondness for fables and fairy tales. Also, collections of miniature fiction have themselves been receiving critical acclaim: Amy Hempel's *Collected Stories* (2006) was cited as one of *The New York Times* Ten Best Books of the year, and Lydia Davis's *Collected Stories* won the International Booker Prize in 2013; prior to that she was a PEN/ Hemingway Award finalist for her collection *Break It Down* in 1986, and a National Book Award Fiction finalist for *Varieties of Disturbance: Stories* in 2007, all of which are comprised principally of flash-length stories. Successes of this kind demonstrate the extent to which the form has been embraced by the literary establishment over recent years.

Understanding the Flash Phenomenon

Miniature stories have become more popular than ever over the past thirty years: outlets for the form continue to grow, and it has a developing presence on the literary landscape. The emergence of new technologies has clearly played a part in this as we have seen, but there are other factors that might have helped create the conditions for its emergence, particularly in America. As early as the mid-1980s, for instance, the novelist John Barth noticed a move toward minimalism among some American writers, which includes what he saw as an increasing interest in brief fiction. According to him there are several potential reasons for this, one being the legacy of the Vietnam War and the tendency for some fiction writers to pare down their narratives in ways that reflect the emotional response veterans often have to conflict:

> Our national hangover from the Vietnam War, felt by many to be a trauma literally and figuratively unspeakable. 'I don't want

> to talk about it' is the characteristic attitude of 'Nam veterans in
> the fiction of Ann Beattie, Jayne Anne Phillips and Bobbie Ann
> Mason[79]

As Barth points out, this was certainly a factor in shaping Hemingway's aesthetic after World War I – his unadorned, laconic style reflects assumptions about masculinity and the importance of managing excessive emotion, not to mention a distaste for the duplicitous rhetoric of those who start wars in the first place. While it is difficult to say whether the Vietnam War created similar preferences among writers, it undoubtedly had a profound effect on American society and culture, and of course there are many veterans of that conflict who produced memorable flash pieces, including Tobias Wolff and Tim O'Brien: indeed the latter's Vietnam-based 'Stockings' appears in *Flash Fiction: 72 Very Short Stories* (1992), the first anthology to use the term flash fiction in its title. Barth also argues that the modern preference for narrative economy registers a reaction against perceived American excesses at the end of the century, particularly in the 1980s, the decade when flash fiction began to take off. He mentions too the decline in literacy in the States both among children and teachers, the reduction in attention spans, and the development of 'a society whose narrative-dramatic entertainment and tastes come far more from movies and television than from literature' (Barth, 1).

The popularity of miniature fiction must also be seen in the context of postmodernism. Whilst some postmodernist writers –

---

[79] Barth, John, 'A Few Words About Minimalism', *The New York Times*, Section 7, Column 1 (28 December 1986) 1
https://www.nytimes.com/books/98/06/21/specials/barth-minimalism.html

such as John Barth himself – are associated with voluminous novels, others such as Donald Barthelme have embraced shorter forms. In his article on minimalism, Barth quotes Barthelme's famous line, 'The fragment is the only form I trust', which might be said to express the attitude many postmodern writers seem to have. Jean-Francois Lyotard discussed the issue of postmodernism in terms of an increasing scepticism toward grand narratives. In *The Postmodern Condition* he wrote:

> We no longer have recourse to the grand narratives – we can resort neither to the dialectic of Spirit nor even to the emancipation of humanity as a validation for postmodern scientific discourse. But ... the little narrative ... remains the quintessential form of imaginative invention.[80]

Lyotard sees a weakening of trust in both metaphysical and secular grand narratives which no longer have power to legitimise our ideas and values. We are less likely to give credence to all-encompassing explanations because we have lost faith in their ability to contextualise and explain our increasingly complex and contradictory world. In the modern world such narratives make us uneasy because we associate them with essentialism, imperialism, totalitarianism, and fundamentalism. For Lyotard this scepticism toward grand narratives is matched by a privileging of the 'little narrative'. We have more faith in brief, tentative, or fragmentary assertions that do not purport to explain everything, but only claim validity on their own terms. This is why irony has been a key feature of postmodernism, because it allows writers to

---

[80] Lyotard, Jean-Francois, *The Postmodern Condition: A Report on Knowledge* (Manchester: Manchester University Press, 1984) 60.

make qualified rather than totalising statements. But such scepticism might fuel the increasing preference for narratives that are 'little' in the literal sense. Ostensibly the ambitions of flash fictions will always seem modest compared to longer stories: they are less likely to have the kind of completist, absolutist feel of longer stories. Thus our enjoyment of miniature narrative might reflect our reluctance to believe in the possibility of a complete, comprehensive story ...

The Poetics of Flash Fiction

The brevity of a story inevitably impacts both on its reception and on its shape. When we read a flash fiction, for instance, we know that it won't take us long to do so – very often we can see the end on the same page – and this surely influences the intensity of our engagement with it. We are more likely to pay attention to the words in a very short story than we might in a longer piece. As a result the words – ie the specific lexical choices – become more important both for readers and writers. Brevity also impacts on what it is possible for a writer to do in the narrative, of course: it affects the form of the story, and that is what I would like to discuss here.

Like Ordinary Short Stories?

Before considering the narrative characteristics of flashes, it is worth considering the features of the conventional short story and how they differ from, say, novels. Addressing the short story in general,

Viorica Patea points out that shorter narratives are more likely to be 'cryptic and elliptical' than novels because they don't allow thorough explanation: 'the reader's intuitions of an unresolved and unstated reality [...] become amplified in the absence of explanatory elements' (Patea, 'The Short Story', 15). The lack of space for detail also means that they are more likely to emphasise 'stylisation' over realism than is the case with novels. They are also more likely to be fragmented than continuous because they preclude the construction of elaborate connections. Short stories tend to be constructed around single moments of disclosure or consciousness too, and this is rarely the case in novels: 'the fundamental element of the short form resides not in narrative structure but in "the moment of truth" or of a crisis conducive to a heightened awareness, a momentary realization that marks the passage from ignorance to knowledge' (15). While Patea is talking about conventional short stories here, it could be said that most of these features apply to flash fictions too. Consider this story from Sterne's 1996 *Microfiction* anthology:

> 'Strongman' – Wendy White-Ring
>
> He can't sleep. He flicks on the reading lamp, lifts the telephone book from the bedside table, takes two deep breaths, and rips the directory lengthwise with three quick jerks. Like yanking the drumsticks off a turkey. 'Order a glass of milk,' I tell him.
>
> Instead, he puts on silver oven mitts, picks up a deck of cards, still in the box, and tears them in half. He breathes in short bursts, as if he's revving a motorcycle's engine.
>
> At home when he's restless, he does arm curls using our golden retriever. Then, with a rope, he drags the van, loaded with our kids, up and down the dark street until sweat softens his muscles the way coarse grass turns limp with dew.

> In this hotel we are two time zones away from our house. So when he asks, 'Just a set', rubbing his arms that are as big around as my thighs, I say OK because even his nose looks wild.
>
> I lie on the floor, my arms straight by my ears. He grabs my wrists and ankles, stands upright, and lifts me to his shoulders. When he pushes me over his head, I see the shape of Florida in an acoustical ceiling tile. 'One,' I count.
>
> In the morning, housewives from coast to coast will watch *The Magnificent Mighty Muscle*, who, using only his longest finger, will balance a famous television talk show host above his head. Yet for now he is simply a man whose hands tremble not from my weight but from all that he cannot clean and jerk.[81]

I would say that this story, just like conventional short stories as Patea defines them, is cryptic, stylised, and fragmented, with an emphasis on a moment of truth. For instance, the point of this story is obvious in one sense but cryptic in others. It is primarily about how this so-called strongman is in fact weak, and its meaning is obvious in this respect; but the implications of this weakness are less obvious. We don't know much about the husband except that he is obsessed with bodybuilding: we don't, for instance, know about his connection with the speaker except that he's the father of her children; we know little of their relationship besides what we can infer from the fact that she does what he asks her to do ('Just a set'), and he doesn't do what she asks him to do ('Order a glass of milk'). Hence it is a snapshot or fragment of their lives that is *necessarily* cryptic – it raises questions because it is incomplete. Are we, for instance, justified in feeling uneasy about their relationship based on the little we know? She decides to obey

---

[81] White-Ring, Wendy, 'Strongman', in Stern, Jerome, *Micro Fiction* (London: WW Norton & Co, 1996) 106-7

him because 'even his nose looks wild', which might point us in the direction of a potentially dark theme, but we can't be sure. So there is an element in the story that remains a mystery, and perhaps adds a degree of nuance to the 'moment of truth' revealed at the end. This 'moment of truth' is that his title, 'Strongman', is ironic, but the cryptic elements create an interesting extra dimension. Still, 'the moment of truth' is quite clearly the insight around which the piece is structured, as in many conventional short stories. The piece is also discontinuous in that it presents abrupt shifts in location, from home, to hotel, to TV studio, without much contextualisation. The story seems in keeping with Patea's point about stylisation too. The author relies on unsubtle, comic imagery to render the scene: the reference to him using the golden retriever as a set of weights is comic rather than realistic, for instance, and both the Strongman and the chat show he appears on plainly invoke stereotype. In short, all of the characteristics that Patea identifies in conventional short fiction are discernible here.

A Poetics of their Own

William Nelles, however, suggests that *very* short stories tend to display different characteristics to conventional short stories. When narratives fall below 'about seven hundred words' he argues that they 'exhibit qualitative differences' from longer short stories.[82] Nelles identifies six principal dissimilarities between short and very short stories: these have to do with action, character, setting, time, intertextuality, and closure, and I'll consider each in turn.

---

[82] Nelles, William, 'Microfiction: What Makes a Very Short Story Very Short?', *Narrative* (Vol 20, No. 1, January 2012) 91

For Nelles there tends to be more emphasis on action in flash fictions: flashes, at least the shortest ones, are mostly constructed around an obvious crucial event rather than reliant on understatement. Understatement and subtlety depend on a narrative's ability to facilitate a greater degree of character engagement than is possible in the briefest stories: in conventional stories a character's feelings are likely to take precedence over action, but the latter dominates in short flashes. We might argue that this is true in 'Strongman' which is governed by two events: firstly, Strongman lifting his wife above his head and, secondly, Strongman lifting the talk show host. Because the speaker's thoughts and feelings aren't fully developed, we might say they are subordinate to these events.

The second difference for Nelles is that characters are less rounded in briefer flashes: they tend to be two, rather than three dimensional, and this is certainly true in 'Strongman'. Here none of the characters are named, and we have very few character indicators that might add variegation to our impression of them; none have psychological depth, and even the character whose thoughts we share is flat.

The third distinction has to do with setting: Nelles argues that the briefest stories move toward the general rather than the particular when describing the setting for the action. Again this can be seen clearly in 'Strongman' which presents an extremely generic hotel room with 'reading lamp', 'bedside table', and 'telephone directory'. The only distinguishing feature is 'the shape of Florida in an acoustical ceiling tile', and even this feels like a token specific detail.

The fourth difference can be seen in the way time is handled: according to Nelles, the duration of short flashes tends to be brief; and when broader timespans are introduced 'writers find inventive ways to keep the duration compressed' (93). Again 'Strongman' is typical of flashes as Nelles describes them in being contained in the present. While the narrator summarizes some past events, and makes a brief flash-forward mention of the following morning, these references are compressed into the 'now' of the story – a single sleepless night.

The fifth difference can be seen in the use flash writers often make of intertextuality. Nelles makes the point that shorter flash fiction, 'frequently introduces an explicit or implicit intertextual reference, sometimes from literary sources, sometimes taken more diffusely from clichés of popular culture or history' (65). While 'Strongman' is free of obvious literary allusions, it does anticipate some cultural understanding and sophistication on the part of the reader: it assumes knowledge of the talk show format, for instance, and of the clichés associated with a host's behaviour. The narrator doesn't have to elaborate on the kind of cheesy entertainment *The Magnificent Mighty Muscle* will provide, or go to any lengths to justify what would seem bizarre in any other context – a man balancing another above his head with a single finger: these are precisely the kind of 'clichés of popular culture' that Nelles has in mind.

The sixth difference for Nelles has to do with closure: he argues that longer short stories put more of an emphasis on ambiguity than shorter shorts, which tend to wind up with a single point, or a surprise ending:

> But while the short story has come to rely more and more on openness and lack of closure, the microstory seems to have remained relatively 'closed' by comparison [...] Certainly the combination of brevity, flat characterisation, brief time frame, and a single generic setting would combine to limit the writer's options for introducing ambiguities, nuances, and symbolic resonances that function so effectively in most open endings. One additional aspect of the plot of microstories [...] is their frequent reliance on surprise endings, perhaps another consequence of their brevity (96).

Ostensibly, of course, this is the case with 'Strongman' which on first reading appears to be constructed around a fairly obvious single point. However, as suggested above, on closer reading the piece seems increasingly complex and open ended, and I think Nelles's final observation is too much of a generalisation. The point he makes about closure seems convincing in relation to the flashes he discusses in his study, which are mostly simplistic, dialogue-driven stories below 50 words. But it is not hard to find stories of extreme brevity which force us to qualify that observation. Consider the following example from Amy Hempel:

> 'Hostess' – Amy Hempel
>
> She swallowed Gore Vidal. Then she swallowed Donald Trump. She took a blue capsule and a gold capsule – a B-complex and an E – and put them on the tablecloth a few inches apart. She pointed the one at the other. 'Martha Stewart,' she said, 'meet Oprah Winfrey.' She swallowed them both without water.
>
> – Stern, *Micro Fiction*, 100

This would seem to fulfil all of Nelles's criteria, except the last. There is an emphasis on action (swallowing of pills); the character is unnamed and undeveloped; there is no setting to speak of; time is compressed to a few seconds; and the intertextual references to popular culture require assumed knowledge. However, few readers would describe this as a closed story. How are we meant to interpret the naming of the capsules after celebrities, for instance? The celebrities she chooses are icons of American popular culture, of course, and the fact that she connects them to vitamins alludes to the kind of health crazes championed on talk shows like *Oprah*. That the protagonist acts as a hostess-of-capsules perhaps implies that she is unbalanced, and hence the story signifies both health (via the reference to vitamins) on the one hand, and pathology (via the character's potential mental illness) on the other. Either way, the story seems completely open: indeed, it depends on ambiguity for its effects. It is successful partly because it invites the reader to try and decode it, hinting at meanings that are ultimately impossible to identify. It is pleasing because the parallel she draws between celebrities and vitamins seems simultaneously incongruous and appropriate; the fact that we cannot say exactly *why* it's appropriate adds to, rather than detracts from, the force of the piece.

The Enigmas of Confinement

Irvin Howe in his introduction to *Short Shorts: An Anthology of the Shortest Stories* (1982) says that 'short shorts are [...] like most ordinary short stories, *only more so*.'[83] He feels that they have the features of conventional short stories, but these are thrown

---

[83] Howe, Irvin, 'Introduction', *Short Shorts: An Anthology of the Shortest Stories*, Howe, Irvin and Howe, Ilana Wiener (Boston: David R. Godine, 1982) ix-xv (x)

into relief by the brevity of the flash-length narrative, creating significant differences. There tends to be a shift of emphasis from character to situation, for instance, in the manner that Nelles suggests, and 'the representative condition tends to replace individuality' (x). However, for Howe the brevity of flashes also augments their potential for mystery: they are more likely to employ 'devices of economy' such as 'oblique cues' in order to replace 'action, dialogue and commentary' and in this way they become '[c]ryptic and enigmatic' (xiii) in ways that are incompatible with Nelles's point about closure:

> Could we say that the short short is to other kinds of fiction somewhat as the lyric is to other kinds of poetry? The lyric does not seek meaning through extension, it accepts the enigmas of confinement. It strives for a rapid unity of impression, an experience rendered in its wink of immediacy. And so too with the short short (xii).

In my opinion Nelles's remarks about closure apply mostly to the least successful flashes: those relying too heavily on surprise, or punchlines; the more interesting flashes exhibit what Howe terms 'the enigmas of confinement' – their brevity creates the conditions for mystery and ambiguity which authors can exploit for their art. Consider this famous flash by Enrique Anderson-Imbert:

> 'Taboo' – Enrique Anderson-Imbert
>
> His guardian angel whispered to Fabian, behind his shoulder:
>   'Careful, Fabian! It is decreed that you will die the minute you pronounce the word *doyen*.'
>   'Doyen?' asks Fabian, intrigued.
>   And he dies.
>
>   – cited in Nelles, 93

On first reading, the impact of this flash appears to be derived solely from the surprise ending – it seems to be closed for exactly the reasons Nelles suggests (in fact Nelles cites it as an example in his article). However, because of the story's concision, the choice of words becomes much more significant than might be the case in a longer narrative. We are inclined to seek a meaning beyond the surprise, and we do so via the 'oblique cues' that we find. For instance, as so often in flashes, the title hints at a subtext, and we might ask how we are meant to interpret the story in relation to the word 'Taboo'. Should we see Fabian's slip-up as indicative of the human susceptibility to temptation: like Eve in the Garden of Eden, will our predisposition for forbidden knowledge always outweigh our capacity for repression? Of course, in such a fleeting narrative the word 'doyen' becomes heavily significant too. Why that particular word? The brevity of the piece throws this detail into relief, possibly even sending readers to a dictionary in order to double-check its precise meaning(s), and etymology. The word 'doyen' refers to a senior member of group: an individual *made* senior either by age or experience. Has it been decreed that death will somehow confer seniority on Fabian? Are we meant to read this symbolically – do men only mature with death, or when the full extent of their own stupidity is revealed to them? However we choose to read it, it is clear that this miniature story is potentially complex; like the best flashes – ie those that tend to endure and invite critical reflection – it is *not* closed.

The capacity for ambiguity strengthens the links between flash fiction and poetry – like the best poems, the best flashes are more than the sum of their parts. In a general discussion of the short story form, for instance, A.L. Kennedy suggests that short story writers enter the realm of poetry because words take on an importance they simply don't have in longer narratives:

> you're certainly in the kind of territory that poets have appropriated, where every word counts on the page. The demands are very similar; you have to have the musicality because it's short, you have to have the shape on the page working because it's short, you have to have these boiled down beautiful multi-layered descriptions of things because it's short. Every metaphor and simile has to work because it's short.[84]

Again, I would suggest that, the shorter the story, the more significant such issues tend to become. Not only does more thought need to go into the potential connotations of the chosen words, as with 'doyen' above, but their shape and sound take on increasing import, as do the appropriateness and fluency of their combinations. Brevity cannot accommodate superfluity, clumsiness, or obviousness.

The Cumulative Effect of Flashes

Flash fictions generally exist as standalone stories, but writers sometimes exploit the possibilities of miniature narrative within bigger frames. When presented as a series of fragments, flashes can be employed to create interesting cumulative effects. Flashes can be themed around places and/or character, for instance, as with recent examples like Sandra Cisneros's *The House on Mango*

---

[84] 'Small in a Way That a Bullet is Small', in Cox, Ailsa, (ed), *The Short Story* (Newcastle upon Tyne: Cambridge Scholars Publishing, 2008) 5-6

Street (1984), and Mark Budman's *My Life at First Try* (2008), two semi-autobiographical flash sequences that use a series of miniature narratives to explore identity. Both of these are discussed in a useful article by Laura Tansley, where she offers an excellent summary of how miniature narrative functions in sequence:

> The short-short, with its characteristic speed and focus, has pace that, when utilised in a sequence, creates a series of steep dives; rapid falls into moments that are read for their precise details and by what is implied. They are short, sharp, stabs of story, their brevity insisting on investigating the very things, the very bare bones of what make up a story. The short-short is marginal, existing on the boundaries of the short story and prose poem, and a boundary is a nebulous place, simultaneously inside and outside. So the short-short is often duplicitous, difficult to place as distinctly one thing, rather than another. And the short-short sequence or cycle comes to exemplify the blurred lines and fragmentary nature of experience in a form that deals with boundaries – the lines that separate one town from another, one person from another.'[85]

Geoff Ryman's *253* (1998) is a good example of a sequence that incorporates some of the features Tansley identifies. The book lists character profiles of 252 people making a single journey between Embankment and Elephant and Castle on a London Underground train. The characters are introduced one by one in narratives of 253 words that include a physical description, details of their occupation, and an account of what they are thinking. The book also provides seating plans for each of the seven carriages so that

---

[85] Tansley, Laura, 'The frame within a frame: a short-short story sequence theory in a sequence of short-shorts', *Short Fiction in Theory & Practice*, Volume 1, Number 1, January 2011, 37-45 (39)

readers can locate the characters and orientate themselves within
the train. Here is an example of one of the profiles:

> 'Mr Richard Tomlinson'
> *Outward appearance*
> Stocky, middle-aged man, athletic build. Rumpled face, very
> pink, with pure white hair. Blue jeans, anorak, woolly red hat.
> He seems lost in thought.
> *Inside information*
> He is returning from hospital having failed to convince them
> to let him die. This is his second bout of pneumonia and he has
> survived three suicide attempts. One left him in a wrecked car,
> sick but alive, in the pouring rain at one in the morning. None of
> his friends know he is ill – except one, Passenger 235, who
> withdrew from him in fear and disgust. Richard lost heart after
> that.
> *What he is doing or thinking*
> Dying is a full-time job. Politics never let up. Richard had the
> support of one doctor, but after a battery of interviews, they
> decided to offer him two more years of declining life.
> Richard's anger at the hospital is cold, shaped by logic. It is
> not for them to tell him he must live. They have not had anal
> herpes that feels like a lighted match on an open wound. They
> have not had the giddy spells, the eye infections, the thrush. As
> far as possible he wanted a normal life. That is no longer possible.
> The best they could do is let him go home. Despite his size, he
> is very weak and cannot breathe. He has just enough strength
> left to walk from the tube, and draw the curtains and listen to
> Mozart and let the pneumonia blossom. An answer machine will
> take all his calls.
> He goes on to Elephant and Castle.[86]

Like most of the character profiles in the book, this works as a

---

[86] Ryman, Geoff, *253* (London: Flamingo, 1998) 55

self-contained flash. The character is suffering from Aids and is suicidal after being shunned by a friend – presumably his lover – and is now heading home to seek solace in music. It presents what Tansley refers to as 'the very bare bones of what make up a story' in its focus on this character's conflict, and his inability to solve it, except by handing his life over to an answering machine. His predicament is underscored by the fact that he is travelling to Elephant and Castle where the train terminates: thus he will soon reach the end of the line both metaphorically and literally, a detail which gives the segment internal coherence and shape. Thus it works as a standalone piece. However, the reference to another passenger – Passenger 235 – invites the reader to make connections of the kind that exist between people in reality, highlighting 'the blurred lines' between stories that might initially appear discrete. If we pursue the reference to Passenger 235 we find it is a character called Tristan Sawyer, who was indeed Richard's lover, and we see him wondering whether he should call Richard, though he ultimately decides not to bother. The experience of reading the whole reinforces our sense of the uniqueness of the characters and their individual stories, but also of the inevitable associations between them. The book first appeared online, where connections between segments are made via hypertext links (underlined in the quoted text above), whereas they are referenced via an index in the hard copy. Reading the online version feels quite different, of course, as the temptation to explore hypertext connections as they are highlighted is so great that one is less likely to proceed through the sequence in order.

How Short Can a Story Be?

Many discussions of flash fiction begin with a mention of the following six-word story, attributed to Ernest Hemingway:

> For Sale. Baby Shoes. Never Worn.

I have deliberately waited till the end before addressing it, because it feeds in to the question I want to ask here: how short can a story be? The answer depends on how we define stories. Simply stated, a story relates two events that take place in time, where there is a causal relationship – either explicit or implied – between those events.[87] So does this apply to 'Baby Shoes'? Once our imaginations have gone to work on it we might want to say yes: certainly there are implied temporal and causal relationships between the imagined demise of the baby for whom the shoes were acquired, and the advertisement of those shoes for sale. We engage with it as a story by filling in the gaps and, in a sense, creating that story around the limited information we have. To some degree this is how all stories function, of course, with readers bringing their own imaginations to bear on the details they are offered. Given its popularity, 'Baby Shoes' seems to work for people, and presumably this has to do with their emotional response to the implicit events. Readers assume that the advertisement follows the death of a baby, and they are affected by the poignancy of this.

The popularity of this story has been a catalyst for a proliferation

---

[87] For a discussion of the defining characteristics of stories see McDonald, Paul, *Storytelling: Narratology for Critics and Creative Writers* (London: Greenwich Exchange, 2014) 15-19

of six-word stories over recent decades, spawning numerous publications and competitions dedicated to the six-word form. A simple Google search will demonstrate that 'Baby Shoes' is habitually cited as the model for aspiring six-word story writers, and the piece is always attributed to Hemingway. This is curious because, as Frederick A. Wright has demonstrated, Hemingway didn't write 'Baby Shoes'. It was almost certainly created by a playwright called John de Groot who wrote a one act play about Hemingway in which the story appears: *Papa: A Play Based on the Legendary Lives of Ernest Hemingway* (1989). The story became widely read as the popularity of flash fiction developed over the last thirty years, and the attribution to Hemingway became ingrained in the public consciousness. Indeed, the story has almost created a genre of its own, with thousands copying the six-word constraint:

> For example, the editors of SMITH Magazine have published numerous six-word texts online and in a series of books [...] Many other publications such as *Black Book* and *Wired* have done the same ('The Hemingway Challenge'; 'Very Short Stories'). Teachers have incorporated the idea into their lesson plans [...] Other writers have cited the story as an inspiration [...] A government funded arts council runs an annual contest for the best six-word stories from Minnesota and North Dakota.[88]

Wright goes on to argue that the Hemingway link is crucial because it is unlikely that readers would accept 'Baby Shoes' as a story if not for this link to an acknowledged master of the form. Indeed, in his view it is debatable whether the story succeeds on

---

[88] Wright, Frederick A., 'The Short Story Just Got Shorter: Hemingway, Narrative, and the Six-Word Urban Legend', *The Journal of Popular Culture* (Volume 47, Number 2, 2014, 327-340) 333

its own terms. Wright says, '[w]ith only six words, the text provides a challenge to readers expecting such traditional short story conventions as plot, point of view, character(s), setting(s), exposition, rising action, climax, falling action, and denouement.' (336). He feels that 'Baby Shoes' only becomes a story because Hemingway purportedly called it a story. Where few people have heard of John de Groot, Hemingway has the authority to assign status to a narrative that most people do not. The implication is that ultra-short flashes are a little like conceptual art: just as Piero Manzoni can transform a can of his own faeces into a work of art, so Hemingway can consign short-story status on six words.

A short story can be as short as the author decides it should be, then, if the author has sufficient cultural cachet. Another example is the Mexican writer Guillermo Samperio, who produced the narrative equivalent of John Cage's *4'33* score with his flash fiction, 'El Fantasma' (which translates as 'Phantom' or 'Ghost' in English). This story takes the form of a title followed by a blank page! We are inclined to accept 'El Fantasma' as a story, perhaps, for the same reason we accept 'Baby Shoes' – because it has been *called* a story by an internationally renowned, prizewinning author of over twenty-five books. And of course, as with 'Baby Shoes', it only takes a little imagination to turn this into a story. If we interpret the ghost as a manifestation of a deceased individual, for instance, then we have an event (death) followed by another event (haunting); and again, as these have a causal relationship, it seems to exhibit all of the criteria we use to define stories. Given that most people don't believe in ghosts, the blank page that follows the title is wholly appropriate!

Conclusion

At the time of writing, the interest in miniature fiction of all kinds continues to grow. There are a host of publications seeking flash fiction submissions, countless competitions catering for the form, and a plethora of anthologies and single author collections of flashes available. In recent years we have witnessed the appearance of university courses specialising in short forms, presses catering solely for flash collections, and societies devoted to its study and promotion. As we have seen, miniature fiction is nothing new, but its proliferation in our times is a fascinating and, for me at least, welcome phenomenon. For those of us who love stories it is a joy to witness this explosion of interest among both readers and writers.

The flash fiction form can accommodate innumerable storytelling strategies, themes, and styles, but its success tends to depend on the attention authors pay to language: the greatest exponents of flash fiction know the significance of lexical decisions. Like poetry, flashes remind us of how important words are, a point beautifully illustrated by one of the best contemporary flash fiction writers, Etgar Keret, in the following story:

> 'Asthma Attack' – Etgar Keret
>
> When you have an asthma attack, you can't breathe. When you can't breathe, you can hardly talk. To make a sentence all you get is the air in your lungs. Which isn't much. Three to six words, if that. You learn the value of words. You rummage through the jumble in your head. Choose the crucial ones – those cost you too. Let healthy people toss out whatever comes to mind, the way you throw out the garbage. When an asthmatic says 'I love you', and when an asthmatic says 'I love you madly', there's a

difference. The difference of a word. A word's a lot. It could be *stop*, or *inhaler*. It could even be *ambulance*.[89]

Flash fiction writers, like Keret's suffocating asthmatic, understand the value of words; within the constraints of the form they are less likely 'to toss out whatever comes to mind'. Life is too short to permit us to say everything, and the modern world is far too full of distractions to tolerate superfluities. Effective communication, more than ever, means thinking like Keret's asthmatic, and having a respect for words: those who truly respect them understand the importance of economy and focus. Regardless of how we might explain the current interest in flash fiction, for me this is why it is worth cherishing as an art form. Flash fiction eschews excess and is driven by the understanding that, when it comes to storytelling, less is usually more.

---

[89] *From The Girl on the Fridge* (New York: Farrar, Straus, and Giroux, 2008) 3

Selected Bibliography

Comment and Criticism

Chantler, Ashley. Notes 'Towards the Definition of the Short-Short Story', in Cox, Ailsa (ed) *The Short Story* (Newcastle upon Tyne: Cambridge Scholars Publishing, 2008) 38-56. A very useful article from one of the editors of the UK-based journal, *Flash: The International Short-Short Story Magazine*. It addresses the emergence of flash fiction and its links to forms such as parables and folk tales, and sees a connection between the increasing popularity of flashes in the 80s and the dissatisfaction with the master-narratives of Reaganism. He also discusses the distinctions between types of miniature fiction, specifically flash, sudden, and micro fiction.

Delville, Michel. *The American Prose Poem: Poetic Form and the Boundaries of Genre* (Gainesville: University Press of Florida, 1998). As the title suggests this book's focus is on the American prose poem, but it also explores the aesthetics of prose poetry in ways that are of interest to scholars of short fiction. Among the prose poets discussed are several whose work might be said to fall into the flash fiction category, including Russell Edson and Margaret Atwood.

Masih, Tara L. (ed). *The Rose Metal Press Field Guide to Writing Flash Fiction* (Massachusetts: Rose Metal Press, 2009). The emergence of 'how to' books has been concomitant with the popularity of flash fiction over recent years. This is by far the best I've seen, offering short articles on the history and theory of flashes, alongside advice to would-be writers from high profile-exponents such as Robert Olen Butler, Kim Chinquee, and Pamela Painter, as well as editors like Tom Hazuka and Robert Shapard. Tara Masih's long introduction, 'In Pursuit of the Short Short Story', presents a lucid account of the emergence of flash fiction.

Moore, W. Dinty (ed). *The Rose Metal Press Field Guide to Writing Flash Nonfiction: Advice and Essential Exercises from Respected Writers, Editors, and Teachers* (Brookline: Rose Metal Press, 2012). This is the companion volume to RMP's flash fiction 'how to' guide above. In answer to the question, what makes good flash nonfiction, Bernard Cooper suggests that it is 'an alertness to detail, a quickening of the senses, a focusing of the literary lens [...] until one has magnified one aspect of what it means to be human' (x). This could work for flash fiction too, of course, which clearly shares an interest in the small things that can tell us big things about life. Much of the advice offered counts for any short form, regardless of fidelity to lived experiences. Each of the twenty-six contributions offers an approach to writing flash nonfiction, a writing exercise, and an example essay. Again there is a very useful history of the form provided by the editor, Dinty W. Moore, and it is more than a 'how to' book: the collection of sample essays itself constitutes a high quality anthology of flash nonfiction, with work from accomplished practitioners like Lia Purpura, Bret Lott and Barbara Miller.

Rourke, Lee. *A Brief History of Fables: From Aesop to Flash Fiction* (London: Hesperus Press, 2011). This history of fables includes useful material on their structure and origins, and traces the form through the ages. It includes chapters on modern miniaturists like Kafka, Borges, and Bernhard, together with worthwhile comments on how the spirit of fables can be found in the work of contemporary flash fiction writers like Tania Hershman.

Key Anthologies of Flash Fiction

Qi, Shouhua (ed and trans). *The Pearl Jacket and Other Stories: Flash Fiction from Contemporary China* (Berkeley: Stone Bridge Press, 2008). This is a bumper collection of Chinese flash fiction. High-profile Chinese writers such as Lu Xun, Lao She, and ex-Minister of Culture, Wang Meng, rub shoulders with lesser-known talents, but the latter are rarely out of place beside the former. Among the stand-out pieces for me are Ma Xinting's 'Hands', in which a woman's head is held in place by a pair of invisible hands, only to be released without explanation, and Yang Kui's 'Roses' where roses become a metaphor for the irrepressible spirit of Chinese youth.

Shapard, Robert., Thomas, James (eds). *Sudden Fiction: American Short Stories* (Salt Lake City: Gibb Street, 1986). In some ways this is a seminal anthology in the history of flash fiction – one of the first modern collections of miniatures to include writers' reflections on the genre, and the first of a series of books collecting short forms both from the U.S. and internationally. Confusingly, the term 'sudden fiction' is still occasionally used to describe fiction that is slightly longer than flash fiction, reflecting the longer word length of the stories here (maximum five pages). It includes work from numerous members of the American canon including Donald Barthelme, Langston Hughes, Bernhard Malamud, Grace Paley, and Tobias Wolff.

Shapard, Robert., Thomas, James., Gonzales, Ray (eds). *Sudden Fiction Latino: Short-Short Stories from the United States and Latin America* (London: W. W. Norton & Company, 2010). With an upper word limit of 1500, this anthology collects writing by Latin American authors and American authors of Latin American descent. It seems to have emerged in recognition of the fact that, in the editors' words, 'The Spanish speaking world leads the way with literary and theoretic discourse in mini and micro fiction.' It includes authors of global renown like Gabriel García Márquez, Isabel Allende, and Jorge Luis Borges, together with less well-known and emerging writers, and it offers a tremendously diverse range of Latin American flashes. It also has a valuable introduction from the avant-garde novelist and short story writer, Luisa Valenzuela.

Stern, Jerome. *Micro Fiction* (London: WW Norton & Co, 1996). Edited by the man who began 'World's Best Short-Short Story' competition in 1986, this anthology is limited to stories below 300 words. It includes finalists from the story contest, plus other work. The book has been a reference point for flash fiction devotees since its publication, and among the better known contributors are, Amy Hempel, James Kelman, and Pamela Painter. It has done much to popularise the term Micro Fiction as one employed to describe the shortest flashes.

Thomas, James., Thomas, Denise., and Hazuka, Tom (eds). *Flash Fiction: 72 Very Short Stories* (New York: W.W. Norton & Company, 1992). This is the book responsible for introducing the term flash fiction. The editors distinguish the collection from the earlier *Sudden Fiction* anthology by reducing the word limit to 750 words. It includes classic flashes like Julio Cortázar's 'A Continuity of Parks', David Foster Wallace's 'Everything is Green', and Richard Brautigan's 'Corporal', among work from high-profile writers like Margaret Atwood, Raymond Carver, Joyce Carol Oates, Tim O'Brien, and John Updike.

Ziegler, Alan. *Short: An International Anthology of Five Centuries of Short-Short Stories, Prose Poems, Brief Essays, and Other Short Prose Forms* (New York: Persea Books, 2014). The distinguished writer and critic Alan Ziegler collects miniature narratives of different kinds here, including flashes, prose poems, brief essays, and 'other short prose forms' embracing fragments, proverbs, maxims, and texts that seem to evade categorisation. It begins with a short section called 'Precursors' which contains early examples of short pieces from people like Michel de Montaigne and William Blake, but the majority of the book covers work from the nineteenth to the twenty-first century. He includes a good selection of shorts from Latin American writers, but nothing from the East. It is one of the most useful and important anthologies of recent years.

OTHER TITLES OF INTEREST

STORY

The Heart of the Matter

Maggie Butt (editor)

978-1-871551-93-8 (pbk) 184pp

W.H. DAVIES

Man and Poet: A Reassessment

Michael Cullup

978-1-906075-88-0 (pbk) 146pp

MILTON'S *PARADISE LOST*

Peter Davies

978-1-906075-47-7 (pbk) 108pp

JOHN DRYDEN

Anthony Fowles

978-1-871551-58-7 (pbk) 292pp

RAYMOND CHANDLER

Anthony Fowles

978-1-906075-87-3 (pbk) 206pp

POETRY MASTERCLASS

John Greening

978-1-906075-58-3 142pp

SWEETLY SINGS DELANEY

A Study of Shelagh Delaney's Work, 1958-68

John Harding

978-1-906075-83-5 (pbk) 204pp

DREAMING OF BABYLON

The Life and Times of Ralph Hodgson

John Harding

978-1-906075-00-2 (pbk) 238pp

WORDSWORTH AND COLERIDGE

Views from the Meticulous to the Sublime

Andrew Keanie

978-1-871551-87-7 (pbk) 206pp

SECOND WORLD WAR POETRY IN ENGLISH

John Lucas

978-1-906075-78-1 (pbk) 236pp

GEORGE CRABBE

A Critical Study

John Lucas

978-1-906075-93-4 (pbk) 220pp

A. E. HOUSMAN

Spoken and Unspoken Love

Henry Maas

978-1-906075-71-2 (pbk)
978-1-906075-73-6 (hbk) 61pp

ERNEST DOWSON

Poetry and Love in the 1890s

Henry Maas

978-1-906075-51-4 (pbk)
978-1-906075-73-6 (hbk) 48pp

POETRY IN EXILE

A Study of the Poetry of Auden, Brodsky & Szirtes

Michael Murphy

978-1-871551-76-1 (pbk) 270pp

DEREK MAHON

A Study of His Poetry

Christopher Steare

978-1-910996-08-9 (pbk) 232pp

BETWEEN TWO WORLDS

A Survey of Writing in Britain, 1900-1914

Hugh Underhill

978-1-906075-55-2 (pbk) 188pp

To find out more about these and other titles visit

www.greenex.co.uk

www.greenexeducational.co.uk